Nott[illegible]
Sherwood Forest

Compiled by
Terry Marsh

Text: Terry Marsh
Photography: Terry Marsh
Editor: Geoffrey Sutton
Designer: Doug Whitworth

Jarrold Publishing ISBN 0-7117-2086-X

First published 2002
by Jarrold Publishing

Printed in Belgium
by Proost NV, Turnhout. 1/02

Jarrold Publishing
Pathfinder Guides, Whitefriars,
Norwich NR3 1TR
E-mail: pathfinder@jarrold.com
www.jarroldpublishing.co.uk/
pathfinders

Front cover: A woodland path near Eakring
Previous page: The lake, Rufford

Contents

Keymap

A61
A6102
Dronfield
Eckington
Killamarsh
DRONFIELD
Holmesfield
Whittington
STAVELEY
Brimington
CHESTERFIELD
Grindleford
Stoney Middleton
A619
A6020
BAKEWELL
BOLSOVER
A617
Holymoorside
Haddon Hall
A6
Rowsley
Northwood
Darley Dale
North Wingfield
CLAY CROSS
Tibshelf
MATLOCK
Matlock Bath
Tansley
Holloway
South Wingfield
ALFRETON
South Normanton
Huthwaite
A38
Middleton
WIRKSWORTH
Brassington
Swanwick
Somercotes
Annesley Woodhouse
A610
RIPLEY
Codnor
A515
ASHBOURNE
BELPER
HEANOR
EASTWOOD
18
Duffield
ILKESTON
6
A52
Quarndon
Allestree
DERBY
Sandiacre
A5111
LONG EATON
A516
A50
Hatton
Chellaston

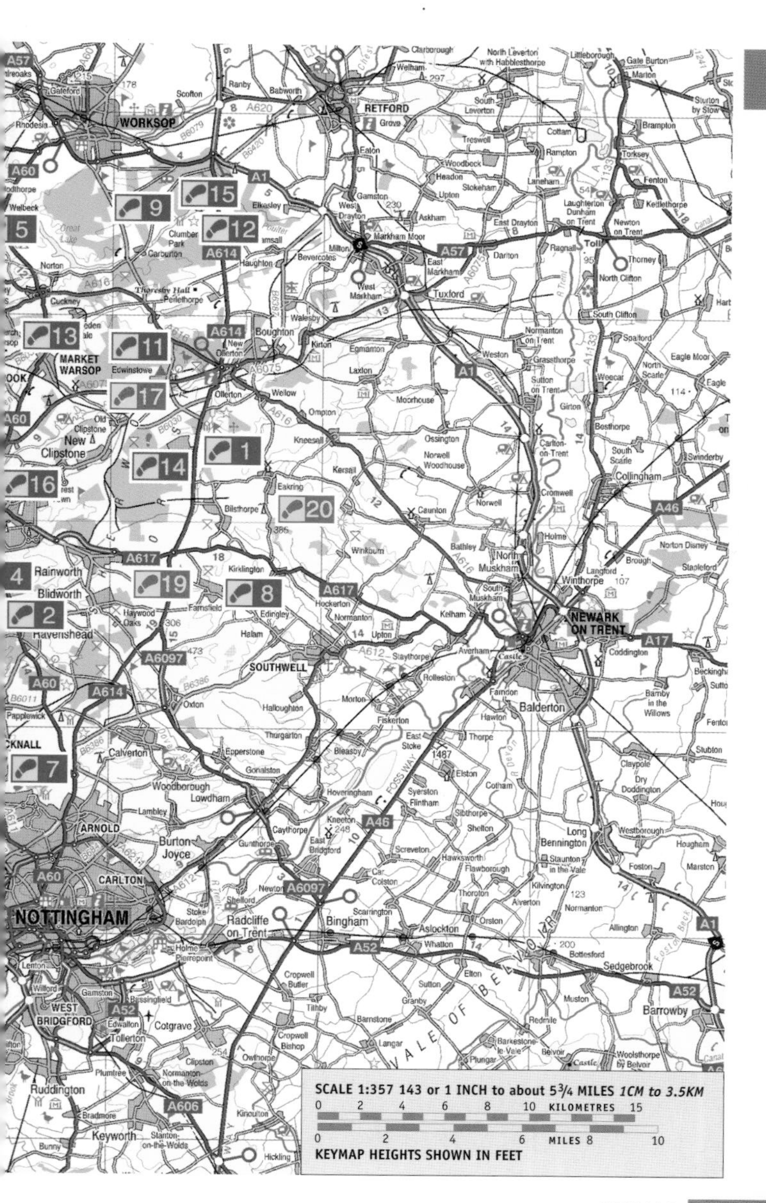
WORKSOP
RETFORD
MARKET WARSOP
NEWARK ON TRENT
SOUTHWELL
NOTTINGHAM
ARNOLD
CARLTON
WEST BRIDGFORD
Bingham
Radcliffe on Trent
Balderton
VALE OF BELVOIR
SCALE 1:357 143 or 1 INCH to about 5¾ MILES 1CM to 3.5KM
0 2 4 6 8 10 KILOMETRES 15
0 2 4 6 MILES 8 10
KEYMAP HEIGHTS SHOWN IN FEET

Introduction

The routes and information in this book have been devised specifically with families and children in mind. All the walks include points of interest as well as a question to provide an objective.

If you, or your children, have not walked before, choose from the shorter walks for your first outings, although none of the walks is especially demanding. The purpose is not simply to get from A to B, but to enjoy an exploration, which may be just a steady stroll in the countryside.

The walks are graded by length and difficulty, but few landscapes are truly flat. Even short walks may involve some ascent, but this is nowhere excessive. Details are given under Route Features in the first information box for each route. The precise nature of the ground underfoot, however, will depend on recent weather conditions. If you do set out on a walk and discover the going is harder than you expected, or the weather has deteriorated, do not be afraid to turn back. The route will always be there another day, when you are fitter or the children are more experienced or the weather is better.

Bear in mind that the countryside also changes. Landmarks may disappear, gates may becomes stiles, rights-of-way may be altered. With the aid of the book and its maps you should be able to enjoy many interesting family walks in the countryside of Robin Hood.

Nottingham and Sherwood Forest

Nottinghamshire lies in the East Midlands, a region of delightful countryside, from undulating farmlands to the dense canopy of Sherwood Forest, legendary 'home' of Robin Hood, England's most colourful folk hero.

The tales of this 'notorious' outlaw are the stuff of legend, yet there is precious little evidence that he actually existed other than a few oblique references in early chronicles. Most of what is known about Robin Hood is drawn from ballads sung during the Middle Ages. Inevitably, these have been adapted so much over the intervening years that the present-day notion of Robin Hood is almost certainly vastly different from reality.

Rufford Abbey

In spite of the mystery that surrounds him, one consensus is that Robin Hood was indeed born at Locksley and was the rightful Earl of Huntingdon: another school of thought suggests he may have been an amalgam of many outlaws, whose deeds and exploits have become welded together. Much of the evidence, however, was based on hearsay, at least until the 19th century, when historians applied themselves to discovering the truth: a truth, however, still without authentication.

In the Middle Ages, Sherwood was a vast, untamed area of woodland and heath stretching from Nottingham to Worksop, having been established as a royal hunting-forest in the 10th century. These 'forests' were for the privileged few and subject to harsh and punitive laws enforced by wardens, known as verderers. The forests had their own 'courts' at which offenders were tried and punished. To be caught within the boundaries of the forest with a bow and arrow, for example, could result in anything from blinding to hanging. To be found with a hunting-dog, meant certain disfigurement both for the owner and the hapless dog.

At the end of the 17th century, 'Dukeries' were created, and their influence significantly altered the landscape of much of the county and produced a nucleus of large estates. Thoresby and Welbeck came first, closely followed by Clumber and Worksop. Here landscaped gardens developed around the ducal mansions.

Elsewhere, the history of Nottingham is told among the acres of the Wollaton estate with its stunning Elizabethan mansion, and at Newstead Abbey, former Augustinian priory and later the ancestral home of the Byron family, which still retains many of the 13th-century monastic gardens. Rufford was founded as a Cistercian Abbey in 1184, and later became the home of the Savile family. Bestwood, once part of Sherwood Forest, was enclosed in 1349. Edward III had a hunting-lodge built here, and royalty frequently used the park, which grew in size to embrace over 3,000 acres (1,215 ha) by the reign of Charles II, who granted it to Nell Gwyn.

Among the county's famous sons Lord Byron is not alone. Novelist D.H. Lawrence was born at Eastwood, Alan Sillitoe, author of *Saturday Night and Sunday Morning* was born in Nottingham, and both J.M. Barrie, creator of *Peter Pan*, and Graham Greene, author of *The Quiet American*, worked on the *Nottinghamshire Journal*.

But it is into the countryside of Nottingham and Sherwood Forest that this guidebook leads. All the walks fall within or border the county and invite an exploration from the heart of the city of Nottingham, where, in

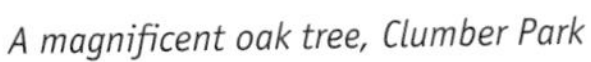

A magnificent oak tree, Clumber Park

Wollaton Park, red and fallow deer graze peacefully, to the wooded precincts of Clumber Park, location of the county's finest church.

Pithead winding-engine house at Bestwood

For lovers of natural history, Sherwood Forest is a tapestry of many colours. Pollen records reveal a history of unbroken woodland cover since the last Ice Age, 11,000 years ago. Inevitably, the forest was exploited for its timber and game and, although the original dimensions of the medieval forest have reduced, there remains enough to give more than a good idea of what life may have been like in the days of the outlaws. More than 900 trees in Sherwood are estimated to be over 600 years old. Some are now distorted into weird shapes, others are hollow but still very much alive, and yet more display the stag-headed outline of aged and dying trees.

Ancient woodlands also mean another fuel, coal. Nottinghamshire has an extensive history of coal-mining. Little of such industry remains today, and the skill with which former mining sites have been reclaimed, restored and redeveloped is to be commended. Local regeneration schemes see to it that once-scarred landscapes are becoming green again, putting back something of what has been lost.

The county is a delight to explore. This book offers to take the reader on a few steps in the right direction – and to hold out the possibility of further, unaided discovery. From farmland to forest, Nottingham and Sherwood Forest have much to offer the inquisitive walker for generations to come.

Woodland • ice-house • historic house and gardens • lake and wildfowl • mill

1 *Rufford Country Park*

START Rufford
DISTANCE 1½ miles (2.4km)
TIME 1 hour
PARKING Main entrance and at Rufford Mill
ROUTE FEATURES Parkland trails; lakeside paths; bridges

In spite of its brevity, this walk has a great deal of interest. At the heart of the park are the remains of Rufford Abbey, founded in the 12th century but later transformed into a grand country-house with attractive gardens and a large lake.

Ornamental detail

From the car park walk towards the abbey ruins and keep to the right of the coach-house building, which today houses shops, toilets and a restaurant.

Rufford Abbey was founded by Gilbert de Gand, Earl of Lincoln, in 1146. Being poor, it was one of the first monasteries to fall foul of Henry VIII's Dissolution, after which it was acquired by George Talbot, Earl of Shrewsbury. Rufford passed to the Savile family in the 17th century. The house fell into disrepair in the 1940s, and much of it was demolished in 1956. Wragby Hall, mentioned in D.H. Lawrence's *Lady Chatterley's Lover*, is based on Rufford.

PUBLIC TRANSPORT Buses to entrance
REFRESHMENTS Restaurant in Coach House
PUBLIC TOILETS In Coach House and at Rufford Mill
ORDNANCE SURVEY MAPS Explorer 28 (Sherwood Forest), Landranger 120 (Mansfield & Worksop)

At the back of the building, near the entrance to the Orangery and the Arboretum, take the path signposted for the Mill, via Lakeside Walk.

At the next main junction **A** turn right for the Mill by the longer of two lakeside walks, and immediately cross a footbridge. A delightful path now follows the edge of the lake to its northern end, and there turns left to reach Rufford Mill.

> The lake was constructed in about 1750 by damming a stream. It proved an attractive feature, and still does, and was used to provide power for the mill, which ground corn. A ford at the back of the mill provides a splash of excitement for children as cars and larger vehicles drive through.

Walk in front of the Mill **B** and shortly turn right to reach the edge of a car park.

Leave the car park by turning left on to the footpath signposted for the Abbey and Craft Centre. Shortly, when the track forks, keep right (signed for the ice house).

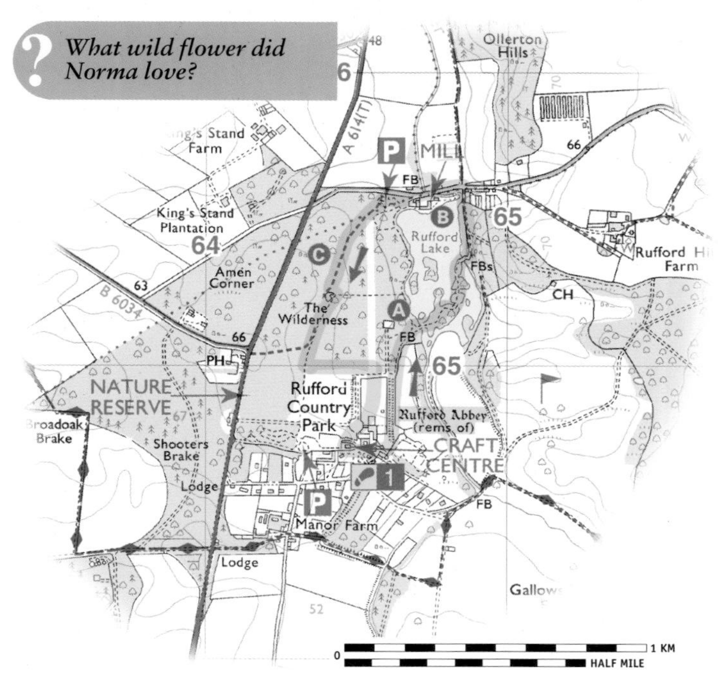

Continue to follow the path past the ice house C. Ice houses were the forerunners of the modern refrigerator, and the idea was first introduced into Britain from the Continent in 1660. There were three at Rufford, all built close to the lake to ease the collection and storage of ice.

The path wanders on pleasantly through woodland. When it reaches a clearing, turn left (signposted the Mill via Lakeside Walk).

At the next signposted path junction, turn right through a hedge gap on to a pathway lined by plane trees around the edge of a large, open, grassed area. Turn right, up steps and then swing left to return to the abbey ruins and the starting point. ●

Feeding the waterfowl in Rufford Country Park

Harlow Wood

START Ravenshead
DISTANCE 1½ miles (2.4km)
TIME 1 hour
PARKING Portland Craft Centre
ROUTE FEATURES Woodland trails

Harlow Wood, and the adjacent Thieves Wood, were used to provide timber for the building of Nottingham Castle, and were largely unchanged until the mid 1970s when storms destroyed many of the mature trees. Today, the wood is a peaceful haven for wildlife, and a pleasant place to walk in the footsteps of Friar Tuck.

Leave the car park and head towards and along a covered walkway running between buildings to the edge of Harlow Wood.

Continue forward past the last of the buildings, soon crossing a track and continuing ahead on a woodland path to meet the route of the Robin Hood Way.

The Robin Hood Way is a delightful 105-mile (170-km) wander through outlaw country linking Nottingham Castle with the village of Edwinstowe on the edge of today's Sherwood Forest – a much smaller version of the medieval forest.

Turn left past a low wooden barrier, and head along a path that ultimately leads into Fountain Dale. Although this walk does not go so far, this is a route that Friar Tuck would almost certainly have taken, as it was here that he first met Robin Hood.

? ***This type of woodland is very popular with members of the tit family. See how many you can spot.***

PUBLIC TRANSPORT Buses along A60
REFRESHMENTS Café at start
PUBLIC TOILETS None on route
ORDNANCE SURVEY MAPS Explorer 28 (Sherwood Forest), Landranger 120 (Mansfield & Worksop)

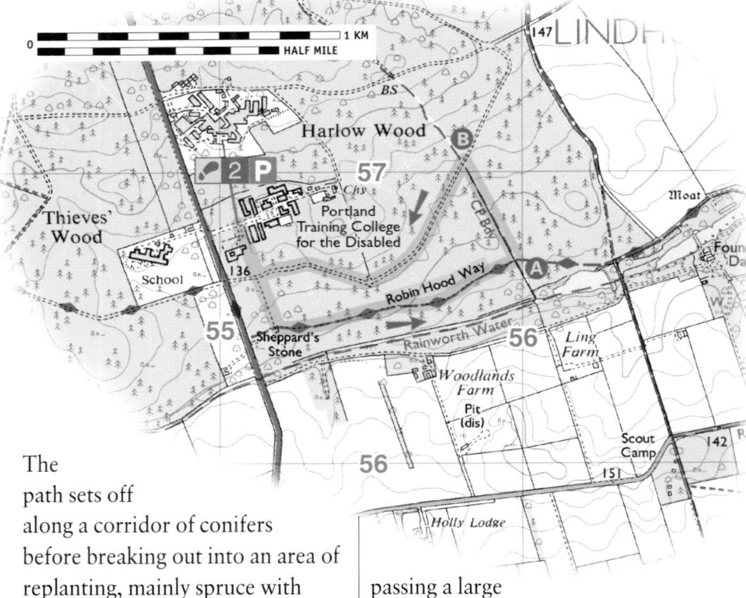

The path sets off along a corridor of conifers before breaking out into an area of replanting, mainly spruce with bracken and silver birch.

When more substantial woodland is encountered, on reaching a broad path **A**, turn left, soon passing a large clear-felled area on the right.

Continue to a T-junction, and there turn left again.

Foxgloves favour path borders in woodland

B Follow the on-going trail, which eventually narrows to become a footpath leading back to the grounds of Portland College.

On reaching the first buildings, turn right to go back along the covered walkway to the starting point.

Wollaton Park

START Wollaton
DISTANCE 2 miles (3.2km)
TIME 1 hour
PARKING Car park at Wollaton entrance (Pay and display)
ROUTE FEATURES Parkland trails; lakeside paths; free-roaming deer

Wollaton Park, opened to the public in May 1929, is the most popular green space within the city of Nottingham, and understandably so. Its 528 acres (214 ha) of parkland, lake and woodland focus on one of the finest Elizabethan buildings in England. Red and fallow deer roam freely in the park and are a delight to watch as they browse on beechmast and acorns.

Wollaton Hall was built in 1580 and completed in 1588. The original builder was a man named Bugge, a wool merchant. He had his name changed to Willoughby after he acquired an estate at Willoughby-on-the-Wolds.

Leave the car park and walk towards the children's play area, and turn right on to a narrow drive lined by oak trees, with Wollaton Hall soon coming into view.

Continue along the drive to a T-junction and there turn right on a gently rising path, towards the hall.

Parkland, Wollaton

PUBLIC TRANSPORT Buses to Wollaton
REFRESHMENTS Snack bar in courtyard
PUBLIC TOILETS At start and in courtyard
PLAY AREA Children's play area adjoining car park at start
ORDNANCE SURVEY MAPS Explorer 260 (Nottingham, Vale of Belvoir), Landranger 129 (Nottingham & Loughborough)

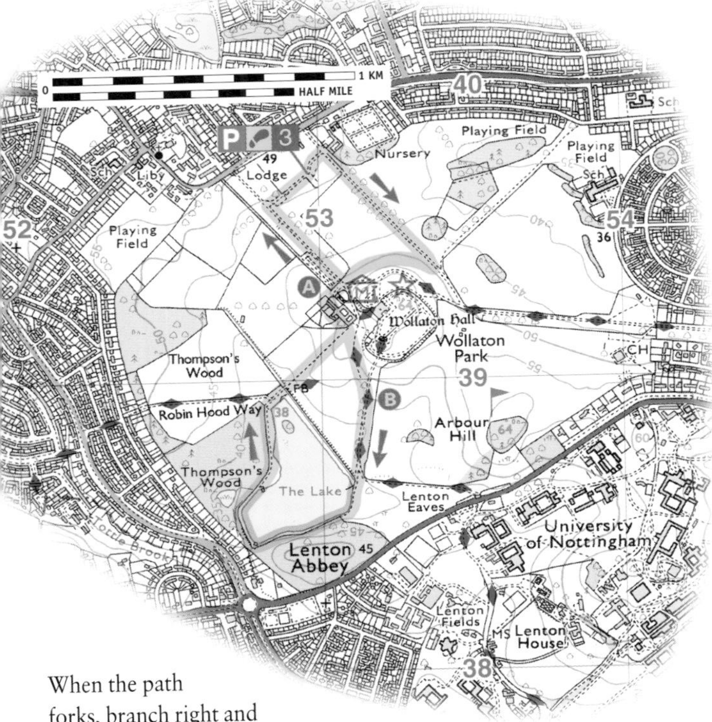

When the path forks, branch right and follow it round to the front of the hall. Ignore the paths leading up to the hall, and maintain the same direction, heading gently downhill towards a telephone box **A**.

Go past the telephone box and turn left into a walled courtyard. Walk through the stables courtyard (toilets here) and on the other side take the second path on the right (the first immediately adjoins the building).

Toni Wakefield was a wife, mother and teacher, and something else. What? Can you find the bench that gives you the answer?

The park has a resident herd of around ninety red **deer** and many more fallow deer. Normally they are docile, but need treating cautiously during June and July when they are calving, and from September to November, which is the rutting season. At these times it is wise to keep a safe distance from them.

The 45-acre (18 ha) **lake** is popular with wildfowl. It was constructed in 1800 from marshland.

Follow the path across open parkland until it feeds into a lime tree avenue leading towards the lake B.

At the far end of the lime tree avenue, when the path forks, branch right, continuing around the lake to Thompson's Wood, a good spot to find deer.

Continue following the lakeside path until reaching a low red brick bridge. Go forward across the bridge and up the avenue of trees, this time flanked by chestnut. This leads back to the stables courtyard.

Turn back through the courtyard and go as far as the telephone box. Then turn left, around the edge of a car park, and walk down another avenue of trees, consisting of a delightful mix of Spanish chestnut, maple, oak, Turkey oak and sycamore. When this forks, turn right to head back to the starting point of the walk.

Wollaton Hall

4 *Thieves Wood*

START Ravenshead
DISTANCE 2 miles (3.2km)
TIME 1 hour
PARKING Parking area just off B6139
ROUTE FEATURES Woodland; route-finding requires care

Thieves Wood is part of the Royal Forest of Sherwood and once was part of the Royal Wood of Lyndhurst, owned by the king. The main route from Nottingham, known as the King's Way, used to pass through Thieves Wood, so it is not unreasonable to suppose that the fate of many travellers gave rise to the wood's name.

Walk through the car park towards a large signpost. Turn left on a route for the Thieves Wood Centre, which is waymarked by blue-banded poles. This is part of the Robin Hood Way (see also Harlow Wood, Walk 2, pages 13–14).

Cross an intermediate track and continue climbing – still waymarked – as far as a broad woodland trail. Turn right along this, still climbing gently.

Somewhere on this walk is 'The Bird Stone', a stone plinth with a carving of a bird on it. Can you find it?

At the next junction **A**, where the Robin Hood Way turns right, keep going forward.

The **wide forest trails** are a pleasure to walk. The woodland is delightfully mixed, including pine, oak and birch. With the trees set back, light gets in and dispenses with the gloominess that often pervades pine plantations. These conditions are also favoured by birdlife, and there are excellent opportunities to spot birds flitting through the trees.

PUBLIC TRANSPORT Buses along B6020
REFRESHMENTS Mobile snack bar at start
PUBLIC TOILETS None on route
ORDNANCE SURVEY MAPS Explorer 28 (Sherwood Forest), Landranger 120 (Mansfield & Worksop)

Daffodils – a sure sign of woodland spring

When the track bends left, leave it by turning right on a path leading down to a picnic area **B**, having left the waymarked route. When the path forks, keep left and about 200 yds (183m) later, branch right on to a narrow path into woodland.

The path flanks a cleared area before heading into woodland and shortly reaches the Robin Hood Way again, another broad forest trail. Turn left.

When the track forks, near a Robin Hood Way waymark, turn right on to a wide path. At a cross-path, turn right and continue to another path junction, here keeping forward.

Eventually, the path meets another wide forest trail. Turn left.

The track now soon becomes a waymarked trail (white-banded poles). Ignore the waymarked trail branching right, and stay on the wide track until it finally reaches the large signpost near the start of the walk.

A scarce aeshna dragonfly

Creswell Crags

START Creswell
DISTANCE 2 miles (3.2km)
TIME 1 hour
PARKING Adjoining Visitor Centre
ROUTE FEATURES Limestone gorge; some road walking; woodland corridor; farm fields

Creswell Crags is a limestone gorge, honeycombed with caves and fissures. Ice Age remains of plants and animals have made the crags one of the most important sites for palaeontology and archaeology in Europe. The caves here are unique time capsules containing many clues to the conditions of life during the Ice Age.

Heavily berried hawthorn

Walk back past the Visitor Centre and take the path sign-posted 'To the crags'. This leads along a constructed pathway that runs beside a stream flowing from Crags Pond. Ignore a bridge on the left and continue, to emerge at the roadside, close by Crags Pond.

? *Evidence excavated in the Creswell Gorge suggests that, in addition to hyenas, there were other, larger mammals living here. Can you tell from information panels what these were?*

PUBLIC TRANSPORT Buses to Creswell
REFRESHMENTS Pub in Creswell; vending machine in Visitor Centre
PUBLIC TOILETS Adjoining Visitor Centre
PICNIC AREA Picnic area near start
ORDNANCE SURVEY MAPS Explorer 28 (Sherwood Forest), Landranger 120 (Mansfield & Worksop)

Go forward along a constructed pathway (although there is an alternative route going left and then right below the base of the crags).

Keep ahead along the path, with crags rising on both sides of the gorge.

One of the caves on the north side of the gorge is known as **Robin Hood's Cave.** It was excavated in 1875 and produced finds of animal bones which show that the cave was used by hyenas and small rodents, birds and bats. Further on, Pin Hole Cave is narrow and about 165ft (50m) in length. The name Pin Hole came from the Victorian tradition of dropping hat pins into a small rock pool at the back of the cave.

When the path reaches the road, turn left and walk out to a T-junction with the A616. Turn right and walk the short distance to a signposted bridleway on the right **A**.

Leave the road and follow the bridleway, going past Bank House Farm. The bridleway is soon enclosed by low hedgerows and climbs gently. Farther on, more established hedgerows flank the

Morning mist at Creswell Crags

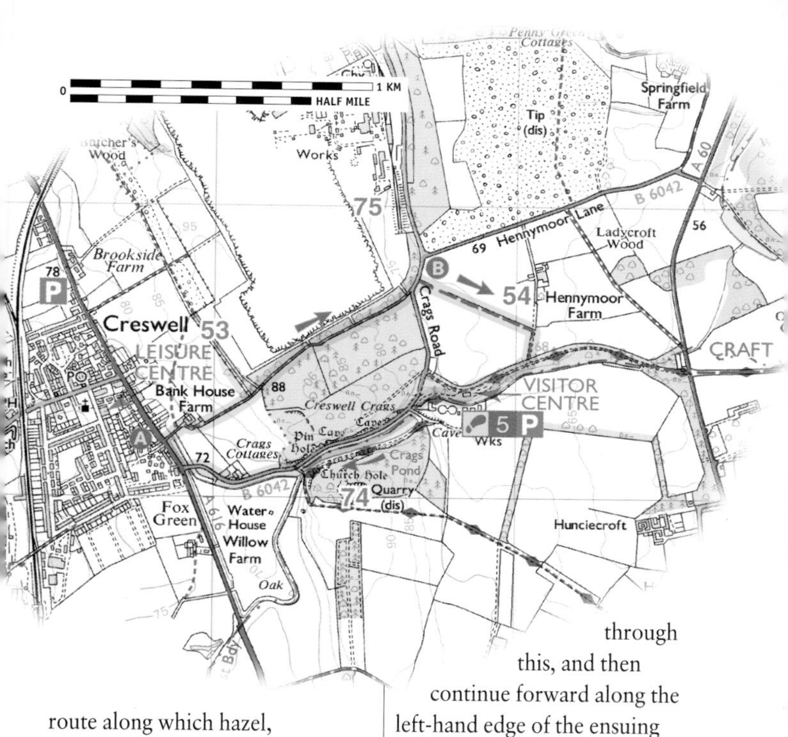

route along which hazel, beech, hawthorn and field maple predominate.

Keep an eye open here for jays, finches and members of the tit family.

The track eventually reaches a road (B6042). Here turn left, but only as far as a hedge gap and gate on the right **B**. Turn through this, and then continue forward along the left-hand edge of the ensuing arable field.

A young ash

The field-edge path runs on to meet a field track. Turn right to enter woodland, and there turn immediately right along a broad track leading back to the visitor centre at the start of the walk. ●

6 Nottingham Canal

START Cossall
DISTANCE 2 miles (3.2km)
TIME 1 hour
PARKING Parking area along Cossall to Trowell road
ROUTE FEATURES Canal towpaths; muddy field

Canal towpath walking is always easy; there are no real gradients. Old canals, long since disused, become colonised by nature and are rich in flora and fauna. This canal is no exception. Even a walk as short as this can produce such exquisite moments as a close encounter with herons or emperor dragonflies.

The **Nottingham Canal** was opened in 1796. It was a mere 14¾ miles (24km) long and ran from the River Trent at Nottingham to Langley Mill at its junction with the Cromford and Erewash canals. It was constructed as a direct route for coal into Nottingham, although it carried other goods too, such as building-stone and grain. After the coming of the railways, the canal became uneconomical; in 1928 it carried no traffic. It was abandoned in 1937.

Leave the parking area and cross a nearby footbridge spanning the canal. Turn right.

After about 200 yds (183m), leave

Farmland adjoining Nottingham Canal

PUBLIC TRANSPORT Buses to Cossall
REFRESHMENTS Pub in Awsworth
PUBLIC TOILETS None on route
ORDNANCE SURVEY MAPS Explorer 260 (Nottingham, Vale of Belvoir), Landranger 129 (Nottingham & Loughborough)

the towpath by turning left over a stile and on to a descending path that leads into a large open field. Strike across this sometimes muddy field, initially aiming for a shallow drainage ditch, and then walk up beside the ditch to rejoin the towpath **A**.

> ? *According to D.H. Lawrence, what traversed the sky?*

Turn left, once more following the towpath. At a prominent track junction, keep forward.

> The canal is especially rich in **wildlife**, which thrives among the reedbeds and stands of bulrushes that have encroached along the canal edge. A patient and quiet approach may well produce the reward of a solitary heron planning its next meal or the darting flight of damselflies and dragonflies, which love this kind of habitat.

Continue as far as the next opportunity to cross the canal, at a small causeway **B**. Here, turn right to return along the opposite bank of the canal.

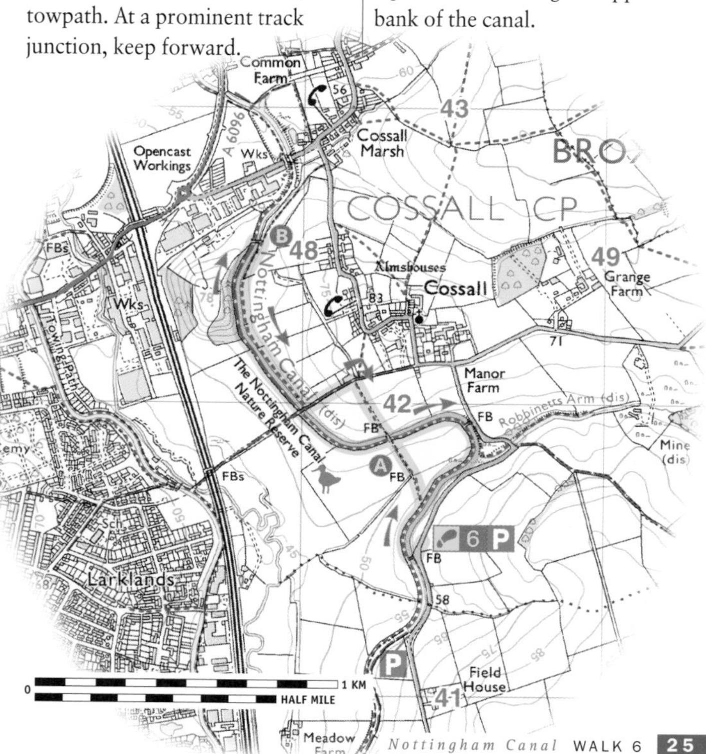

Bulrushes by the Nottingham Canal

On returning to the cross-track, turn left up a leafy lane, but only as far as a signposted path on the right for Trowell and the towpath.

Here, cross a stile, and walk down the ensuing field, keeping to the left of a post and wire fence. At the bottom of the field, recross the canal on a footbridge, and then turn left.

Along this return section, keep an eye open for some interesting **fencing** work on the right-hand side, produced by interweaving branches of hazel to give a strong and durable barrier.

Now follow the towpath all the way back to the starting point of the walk.

Cover pathway, Cossall

● Woodland wildlife ● coal-mining buildings ● extensive views

Bestwood Country Park

7

START Bestwood Village
DISTANCE 2½ miles (4km)
TIME 1¼ hours
PARKING Country Park entrance
ROUTE FEATURES Reclaimed mining area; woodland; some uphill

The site on which Bestwood colliery was built is an ancient one, being mentioned in the 'Domesday Book'. The estate was acquired by Nell Gwyn in 1687, and became the seat of the dukes of St Albans, descendants of Nell Gwyn and Charles II. The grounds were used for military training in the 20th century and used as a regrouping point for survivors of Dunkirk during World War II.

Snowberry, Bestwood Country Park

Leave the car park and turn into the country park, walking to the Winding Engine House and its pithead gear, stark against the sky.

Bear right on to a path that leads across open fields. When the path forks, bear left, climbing a little to meet two parallel trails (one for horses, and a slightly higher one for walkers). Turn right.

When the trail forks, branch left and follow the trail as it climbs gently across a landscape that would once have echoed to the sounds of man's industry.

PUBLIC TRANSPORT Buses to entrance
REFRESHMENTS Pubs in Bestwood
PUBLIC TOILETS None on route
ORDNANCE SURVEY MAPS Explorer 260 (Nottingham, Vale of Belvoir), Landranger 129 (Nottingham & Loughborough)

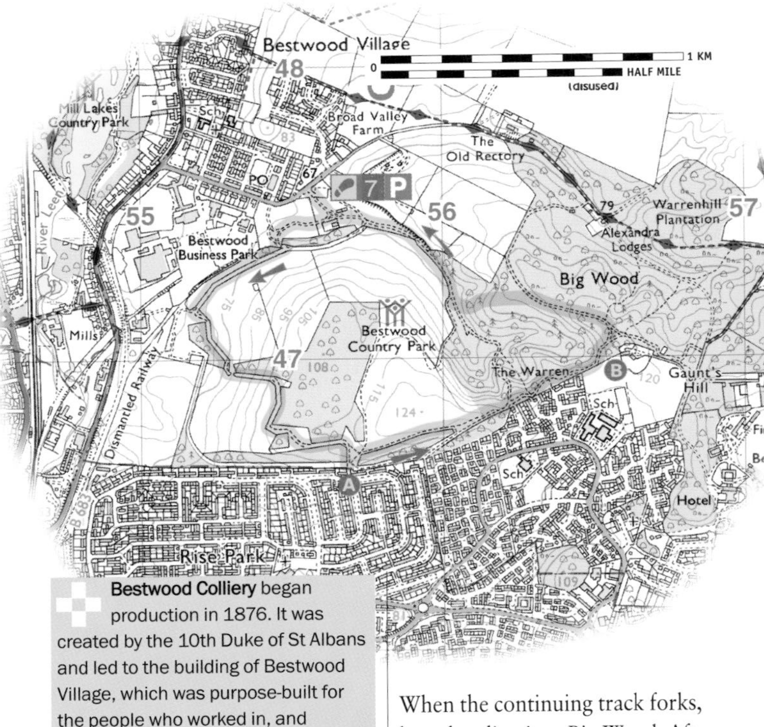

Bestwood Colliery began production in 1876. It was created by the 10th Duke of St Albans and led to the building of Bestwood Village, which was purpose-built for the people who worked in, and depended on, the mine. The pit was closed in 1967, but in its heyday the colliery provided employment for 2,500 people.

The path continues climbing around fenced areas of replanted trees and, eventually, swings down towards a gate giving into a housing estate **A**.

Just before the gate, turn left on a track heading into woodland and signposted for Big Wood and Lodge Gardens.

When the continuing track forks, keep heading into Big Wood. After passing a school playing-field (on the right), the path clearly enters the domain of Big Wood **B**.

More **established trees** now flank the path, including Spanish chestnut, oak, ash, hawthorn and sycamore, all of which provide an ideal habitat for grey squirrels and garden birds like robin, blackbird, song thrush, as well as winter visiting mistle thrush and fieldfare. Keep an eye open across the adjacent fields for patrolling kestrels on the look-out for a quick meal.

In **Big Wood** the trees are more varied, and here include birch and some yew. **Yews** are more commonly found in churchyards, where they can live to be 1,500 years old. They are thought to be sacred and may have first been planted at sites of pagan worship before to the building of a church. They are, of course, woodland trees too.

Keep forward on an obvious path which shortly forks near some low railings. Here, branch left, following a waymarked route.

Continue following the path as far as another junction, signposted to the Winding House. Turn left here and keep an eye open on the left for some stands of snowberry.

The track leads back to the Winding House, at which, turn right and walk back out to the car park at the starting point of the walk.

? *Among the birds that frequent woodlands like Big Wood are members of the tit family. One has an especially long tail. Do you know what it is?*

Autumnal shades in Bestwood Country Park

8 *Southwell Trail*

START Kirklington
DISTANCE 2½ miles (4km)
TIME 1½ hours
PARKING Kirklington car park and picnic area
ROUTE FEATURES Railway trackbed; farm field paths; a few low stiles

This easy walk makes use of a section of an old railway trackbed before striking across farm fields to the small village of Edingley. Springtime flowers and birdlife provide interest, while the raised level of the trackbed affords glimpses over the surrounding countryside.

The **Southwell Trail**, a disused railway line, provides almost 7 miles (11.3km) of track for walking, cycling, horse-riding and picnics. It passes through shaded cuttings and along embankments with views over the surrounding villages and fields. This was once a busy branch line connecting Mansfield, Farnsfield and Ollerton to the line between Newark and Nottingham. The single track was completed in 1871 and transported people, milk, coal and oil. It closed in 1965.

Leave the car park, heading along the trackbed (signposted for Farnsfield).

Continue following the trackbed for just under a mile (1.6km) before leaving it at a pathway branching left into a field **A**. The exact spot is easy to miss, so keep

Much of the route is flanked by hawthorn, beech, ivy, bramble, oak, ash and elder, species typical of railway corridors, but with more varied species across the nearby farmland. They provide a splendid haven for **wildlife**, especially in spring and summer when a variety of birds feed and nest in the dense vegetation. Wild flowers can be found along the embankments and in the adjacent meadows.

PUBLIC TRANSPORT Buses to Kirklington and Edingley (alternative start)
REFRESHMENTS Family friendly pub at Edingley
PUBLIC TOILETS None on route
PICNIC AREA Near start of walk
ORDNANCE SURVEY MAPS Explorer 28 (Sherwood Forest), Landranger 120 (Mansfield & Worksop)

an eye open for it, in particular a grey metal pole standing a few feet beyond the turning.

Go down the path and forward along the right-hand edge of the ensuing field (yellow waymark at start of hedgerow).

About three-quarters of the way down the field, the path bears left to the far corner and a sleeper bridge giving into an adjoining pasture.

Entrance to St Giles' Church, Edingley

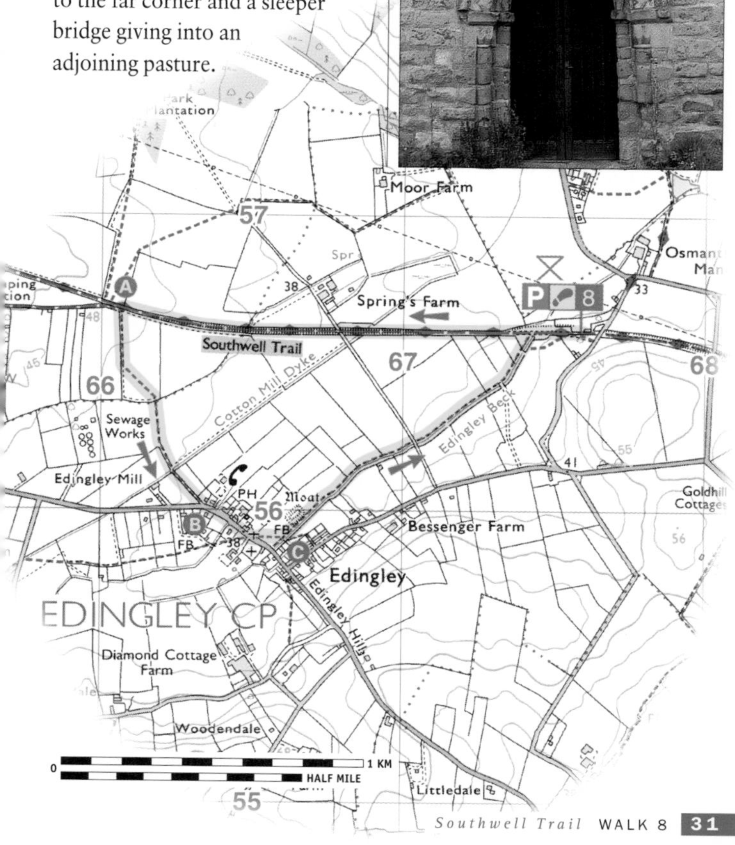

Morning mist on the Southwell Trail

> ***?*** ***Of the many trees found in the British countryside, some seem to appear in churchyards more than they do elsewhere. What are they? And why do you think this is so?***

Head straight across the field, aiming to the left of a central oak tree. On the other side, maintain the same direction along a field track that finally runs out to meet a road on the edge of Edingley **B**.

Turn left and walk towards the village centre, and, directly opposite the parish church of St Giles, leave the road by turning left on to a signposted footpath that immediately cuts half-right, across a field to a footbridge spanning a dyke **C**.

Do not cross the bridge. Instead, keep left, walking alongside the dyke. The path leads to a stile in a field corner. Beyond this, head for another stile, keeping to the same direction.

The path eventually emerges on to a rough stony track. Cross this, going into the next field and following a field-edge path to another corner stile, giving on to a path around a large paddock. Then, go on by a waymarked route across a couple of small fields to rejoin the Southwell Trail. Turn right to return to the start.

Clumber Park

START Hardwick
DISTANCE 3¼ miles (5.2km)
TIME 1½ hours
PARKING Car park north of Hardwick
ROUTE FEATURES Woodland trails; lakeside paths

This brief encounter with the Clumber spends time wandering off into woodland, before visiting a splendid chapel and finishing alongside the lake. Woodland birdlife is plentiful, while the lake hosts a multitude of waterfowl, from swans to tufted duck.

Leave the parking area and walk towards a surfaced access that crosses the lake. Soon leave the road by bearing left on to a waymarked footpath (yellow waymark).

The path soon heads into woodland, where it forks **A**. Keep ahead, following the right branch to a wooden barrier at a track junction. Here turn right.

Just after the next barrier, at another junction, turn left along a surfaced lane. Keep left when the lane merges with another from the right.

Clumber Lake

PUBLIC TRANSPORT Buses along Lime Tree Avenue
REFRESHMENTS Restaurant at Clumber Visitor Centre
PUBLIC TOILETS Near visitor centre
ORDNANCE SURVEY MAPS Explorer 28 (Sherwood Forest), Landranger 120 (Mansfield & Worksop)

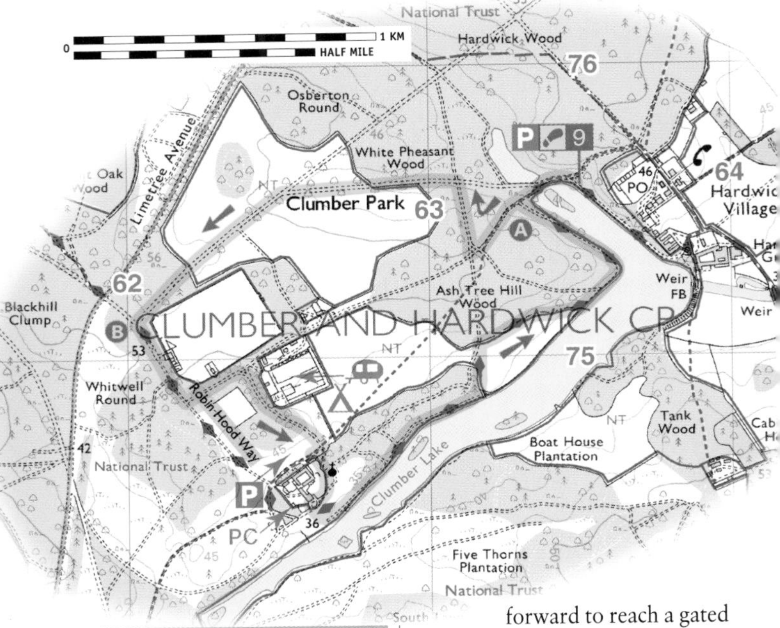

Along the walk two semicircular seats are encountered. Part of their design includes a number of small tile mosaics. How many complete circles can you find in all the designs put together?

Continue to a road junction **B** and there turn left. Walk down as far as a bus shelter on the right and turn left on to a broad track opposite.

When the broad track forks after about 200 yds (183m), bear right, going past the Clumber Conservation Centre, and keep forward to reach a gated entrance into the Victorian Clumber Chapel. Turn in here if you wish to visit the chapel.

From the chapel, walk right, to the shop and restaurant area, and there go left on a paved pathway across a lawned area to meet a path along-

Clumber Chapel is a splendid High Victorian Gothic chapel built between 1886 and 1889 by G.F. Bodley for the 7th Duke of Newcastle. This is a masterpiece of Gothic revival architecture in Runcorn stone and is one of the finest churches in Nottinghamshire, regarded by Bodley as his finest work.

side the lake. Turn left and follow the lake edge.

Keep following the lake-edge path, which leads past two ornate semi-circular seats from which steps lead down to an ornamental pathway.

Towards the end of the ornamental pathway, go down three steps and then immediately turn left into woodland.

A short distance on, keep an eye open for a branching path on the right. Swing right here, following the path to a stone gate arch. Cross between meadows to a pair of gate-posts opposite.

At the gateposts, turn right on to a path alongside a fence, which soon turns into woodland and continues parallel with the edge of the lake.

When the path emerges at a T-junction, turn right to return to the start. ●

A view of St Mary's Church, Clumber

10

Attenborough Nature Reserve

Only a short distance from the centre of Nottingham, the Attenborough Nature Reserve is based around former gravel pits alongside the River Trent. It is a perfect place to watch birds, and a pair of binoculars is a useful item to carry on this walk, which is easy throughout.

START Attenborough
DISTANCE 3½ miles (5.6km)
TIME 2 hours
PARKING Car park at the reserve
ROUTE FEATURES Woodland trails; lakeside and riverside paths that occasionally flood

Leave the car park and walk along a footpath heading in the general direction of the steepled Attenborough Church. The path passes between two large lakes. When it forks, branch right along a causeway.

On the far side of the causeway, turn left over a bridge and walk out to a road. Turn right.

? *Can you find a kingfisher and a duck sitting side-by-side?*

A Follow the road to its end, where it reduces in size to become a bridleway that leads around the edge of another large lake. Continue across a large footbridge and immediately bear left when the

Wrens, robins, great, blue and long-tailed tits love this kind of habitat, and are joined throughout the year by visiting **birds** such as swallows and warblers in summer and brambling and mistle thrushes in winter. Keep an eye open also for cormorants perching on branches in the middle of the lakes, drying their wings, and for breeding pairs of great crested grebes.

PUBLIC TRANSPORT Buses to Attenborough
REFRESHMENTS Pub and tearooms at Beeston Marina
PUBLIC TOILETS None on route
ORDNANCE SURVEY MAPS Explorer 260 (Nottingham, Vale of Belvoir), Landranger 129 (Nottingham & Loughborough)

path forks, walking through light woodland that supports a wealth of birdlife and wild flowers.

The path eventually turns right to parallel a railway line for about 200 yds (183m) and then, near a railway crossing, bears right on to a route waymarked

The River Trent, Attenborough

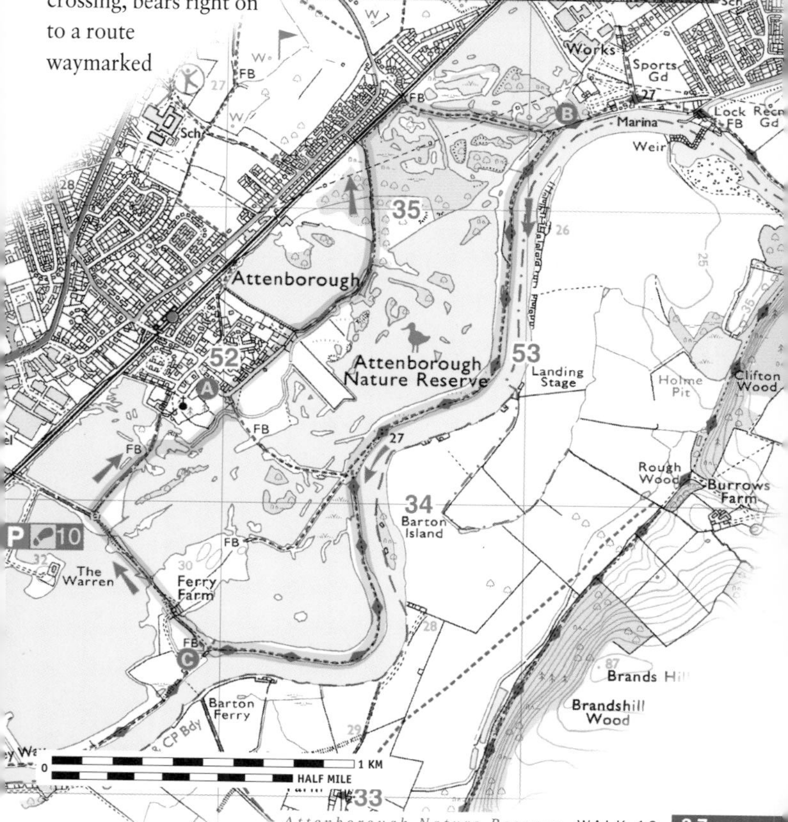

by blue-banded poles. Once more you walk between lagoons, fringed with reeds and bulrushes.

The path eventually emerges on the left-hand bank of the River Trent **B**. Turn right, still following the blue-banded waymarks.

Keep forward across a footbridge where the waters of the nature reserve, fed by the River Erewash, flow vigorously into the Trent. The riverside path is a delight to walk, lined by field maple, hawthorn, oak, crack willow, birch and ash. Keep an eye open for the darting flight of kingfishers that patrol the riverside banks and for woodpeckers in the flanking hedgerows and small woodlands.

Keep following the Trent-side path past Barton Island, and still following the blue-banded waymarks, now paired with red-banded waymarks.

When the path forks **C**, follow the red and blue trails. Walk forward on a broad track that leads over a bridge and back to the starting point of the walk at the car park.

A wide view of the River Trent, Attenborough

● Woodland wildlife ● ancient oak trees ● seasonal fungi

Sherwood Forest

11

START Edwinstowe
DISTANCE 3½ miles (5.6km)
TIME 2 hours
PARKING Opposite Sherwood Forest youth hostel
ROUTE FEATURES Woodland trails, occasionally muddy

This walk is especially pleasing in autumn, when the wood is carpeted with a splendid variety of fungi. In spring, the trees are alive with birdsong, and the woodland shadows patrolled by fleeting roe deer.

Leave the car park and walk towards, and in front of, the nearby fairground, walking on to an improving path, a bridleway signposted for Gleadthorpe. The path soon becomes a broad track along the edge of the forest, with an arable field on the left.

When the far end of the arable field is reached, the track forks. Branch left **A**, still signposted for Gleadthorpe. Almost immediately, go left at a metal barrier on to a path parallel with the woodland boundary.

Continue following the forest-edge track until it enters a wide forest ride at a bench. Here, turn right,

? *What was the first recorded name of the Major Oak?*

It is tempting to suppose that the **Centre Tree** marks the central point of the medieval Sherwood Forest, but though that may be so, it was also used to denote the boundary between the two adjacent dukedoms of Newcastle and Welbeck.

PUBLIC TRANSPORT Buses to Edwinstowe (Forest Corner)
REFRESHMENTS Edwinstowe and café at Visitor Centre
PUBLIC TOILETS Adjoining Visitor Centre
PLAY AREA Adjoining Visitor Centre car park
ORDNANCE SURVEY MAPS Explorer 28 (Sherwood Forest), Landranger 120 (Mansfield & Worksop)

Robin Hood and Little John

walking up the ride, flanked by holly and conifers, to a track junction close by the Centre Tree B.

Go past the Centre Tree, going forward on a broad, grassy forest trail flanked by birch trees.

Keep following the ride until it ends at a

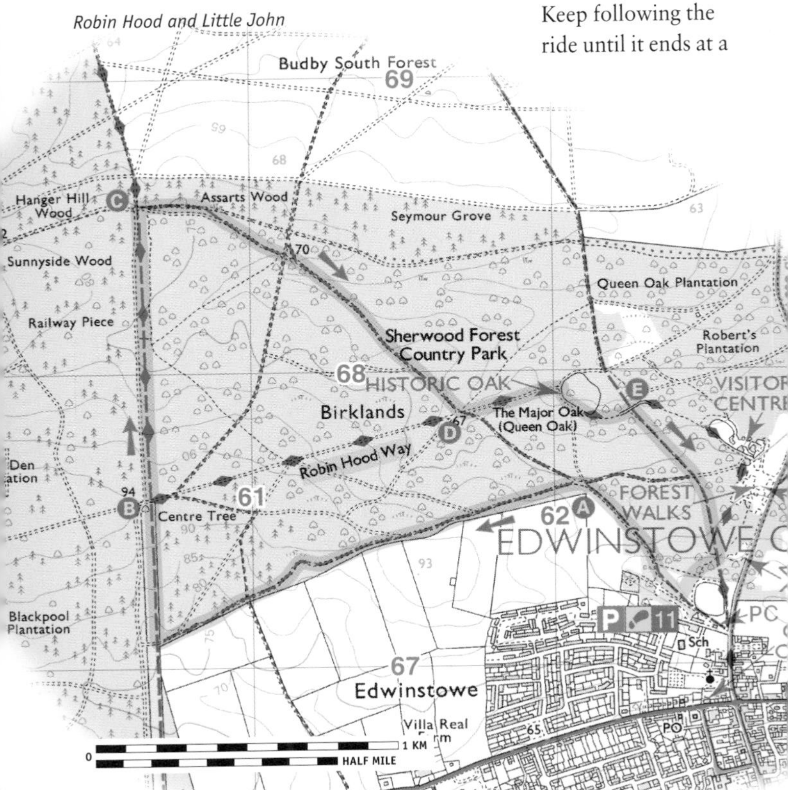

semi-surfaced track, near a metal barrier. Here **C**, turn right on to a bridleway (yellow trail waymark) heading into an area of the forest known as Assarts Wood.

The walk along this grassy ride is especially agreeable, being open and airy but with ample damp and shady nooks to host a wide range of **fungi**, for which the woodland is renowned. Some of these are poisonous, so, in the absence of expert knowledge, it is better to avoid touching any of them.

D Turn left and take the middle of three possible tracks. This leads eventually to a T-junction, with the massive Major Oak standing a short distance to the right.

The path immediately forks. Branch right here, following the yellow trail until it intercepts the red trail, here part of the Robin Hood Way.

Continue past the Major Oak, to follow a broad track between fences. Keep following the track until it crosses a bridleway marked by narrow gates on either side.

The Major Oak in Sherwood Forest

A woodland glade in Sherwood

Turn right here **E**, (anyone wishing to go to the Visitor Centre should keep ahead and later follow the signed path away from the Visitor Centre and back towards the youth hostel).

The **Major Oak**, a penduncluate oak (*Quercus robur*), is estimated to weigh 23 tons, has a waistline of 33ft (10m) and is thought to be about 800 years old. Its canopy has a spread of 92ft (28m). The tree did not become well known until about 200 years ago, when it was mentioned in 1790 by Major Hayman Rooke, who in the same year published a book about amazing trees in this area. A short time later the tree was named after him.

Cross an intermediate track and, when the bridleway forks, keep right.

At its far end, the bridleway emerges through a gate on to a track. Turn right here for the youth hostel, soon heading across an open field towards the fairground and the car park beyond.

The name '**assart**' is a reminder of medieval times when forest life was regulated under stringent forest laws, which included the right of people to collect wood for kindling or roofing and to gather beech nuts for pig food. An 'assart' is an area of woodland cleared for farming.

Clumber Lake

START Hardwick
DISTANCE 3½ miles (5.6km)
TIME 2 hours
PARKING Car park at Hardwick
ROUTE FEATURES Woodland trails and lakeside paths

Clumber Park is one of the most popular places in the East Midlands, a huge 4,000 acres (1,600 ha) of woodland, heath and grassland. It was once the seat of the dukes of Newcastle, but is now owned by the National Trust. The walk circles the beautiful lake and provides many delightful woodland cameos.

The walk begins from the 19th-century estate village of Hardwick. Leave the car park by heading along a short track leading to the edge of Clumber Lake. Turn right, passing toilets, to follow a lakeside track to another car park, beyond which a road is met. Turn left and soon leave the road by bearing left on to a waymarked footpath (yellow waymark).

The path soon heads into woodland, where it forks **A**. Keep ahead, following the right-hand branch and overhead powerlines to a wooden barrier at a track junction.

Clumber Bridge

Go forward, along a broad forest trail that eventually meets a lane (surfaced). Keep ahead past estate cottages and the Estate Office **B**.

PUBLIC TRANSPORT Buses along Lime Tree Avenue
REFRESHMENTS Restaurant at Clumber Visitor Centre
PUBLIC TOILETS At start and in shop area
ORDNANCE SURVEY MAPS Explorer 28 (Sherwood Forest), Landranger 120 (Mansfield & Worksop)

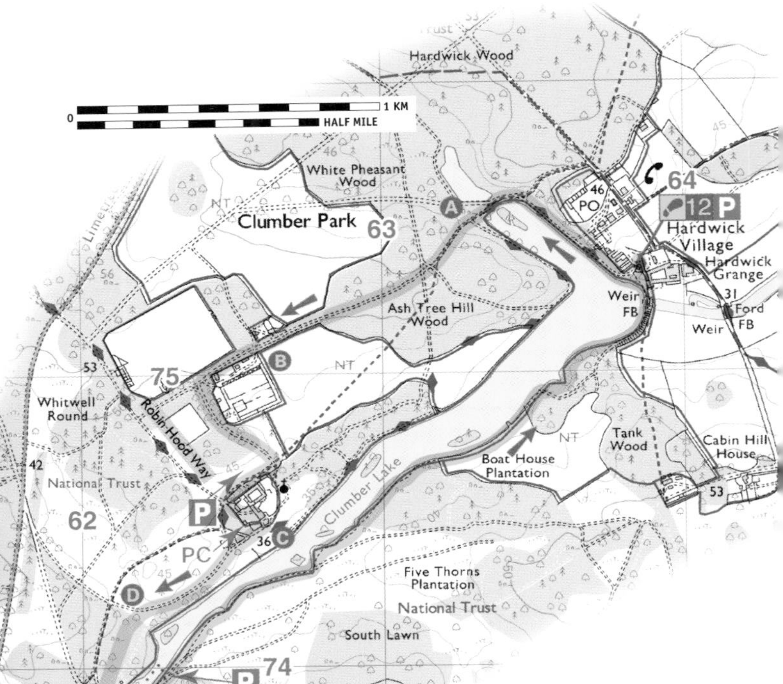

A short distance beyond the buildings, turn left, still on a surfaced lane and passing the Clumber Conservation Centre. The lane eventually leads to the main estate car park.

Who was Diana?

Go past the car park to a road junction, and there turn left towards the shop area, passing between old gate pillars. Keep to the right of the shop and restaurant, go past an information point and on to a paved path across

The **Clumber estate** formed part of Sherwood Forest until, in the early 18th century, the Duke of Newcastle was granted a licence to enclose the area as a hunting-park for Queen Anne. The house was begun in 1767, but was largely destroyed by fire in 1879. Rising costs and taxation caused the house to be abandoned in the 1930s. The magnificent lake was formed from the River Poulter, taking fifteen years to build at a cost of £6,612 8s 9d.

the site of Clumber House and its Italianate Gardens **C**.

The **lake** is host to many species of birdlife, including shoveler, mallard, tufted duck, heron, coot, moorhen, great crested grebe, garganey, mute swans and Canada geese.

Walk towards the lake but, before reaching it, turn right on a surfaced pathway leading into lakeside woodland of oak, beech and birch. Follow the path through the woodland, on the way passing the Clumber Grotto **D**.

Beyond the grotto continue on a clear path until it emerges at a road, close by Clumber Bridge. Turn left over the bridge, an elegant Palladian bridge built in 1770, and immediately go left again on to a lakeside path until it becomes possible to head for a small car park.

Beyond the car park, continue on a broad track parallel with the lake edge.

Continue following the track around the lake to cross a weir and reach Hardwick village. Turn right to return to the car park.

The lake and St Mary's Church, Clumber

• Riverside wildlife • attractive river • farmland

13 *Warsop Vale*

START Church Warsop
DISTANCE 4 miles (6.4km)
TIME 2 hours
PARKING Adjoining Meden Bridge
ROUTE FEATURES Riverside path; farm fields (muddy) and lanes

The River Meden is narrow and shallow, but extremely attractive. It flows through gentle countryside where a quiet approach will increase the chances of seeing the abundant birdlife that flourishes in this open, hedgerowed setting.

Looking back, the village of **Church Warsop** sits attractively around the dramatic Church of St Peter and St Paul. Church Warsop is one of a number of settlements that comprise Warsop and was once an important mining community.

Start from the car park by walking over to the riverside path (do not cross the bridge) and follow it around the edge of a large playing-field. Further on, the river, flanked by extensive displays of willow and alder, meanders gently.

Continue with the path, which later crosses a footbridge, after which it immediately turns right, now along the true right bank of the river (A).

At the next footbridge, leave the river by turning left on to a surfaced bridleway that runs along the edge of a housing estate. Take the first turning on the right (The Hawthorns).

It is sometimes confusing to figure out which bank of a **river** is left and which is right. The solution is simple: face in the direction of the river's flow and the banks are then respectively left and right, and known as the 'true' left or right bank.

PUBLIC TRANSPORT Buses to Church Warsop
REFRESHMENTS Pubs in Church Warsop and Market Warsop
PUBLIC TOILETS None on route
ORDNANCE SURVEY MAPS Explorer 28 (Sherwood Forest), Landranger 120 (Mansfield & Worksop)

At the far end of the Hawthorns, at a T-junction, turn right and soon enter an enclosed sandy lane, which soon recrosses the River Meden at a good spot to watch for kingfishers **B**.

A short way on, the track passes beneath a railway bridge. Continue to follow it, as far as Herrings Farm **C**. Here turn right on to a signposted bridleway that soon dips into a hollow-way (sunken track) between established hedgerows.

River Meden, Church Warsop

Immediately after emerging from the

?

The River Meden is host to many species of birds. One in particular is small, black, with white under-tail feathers, yellow legs and a red beak with a yellow tip. How many can you spot? Do you know what it is called?

enclosed pathway, turn right on a signposted bridleway across arable fields, heading for a railway tunnel.

Beyond the tunnel, head straight across the ensuing field to a gate on the far side. Through the gate, turn left and head for the left-hand corner, at the back of two red-brick houses. Through another gate, turn right and walk out to a road, the B6031.

Turn right and walk alongside the road for about 500 yds (457m), taking care against approaching traffic. Go as far as a signposted footpath on the right and here leave the road by turning on to a narrow, surfaced pathway between low hedges.

The path merges with a bridleway and bears right to a footbridge.

Over the bridge, turn left down steps and at this point rejoin the outward route. Now simply follow the river back to the start.

Church Warsop

● Woodland birds ● deer ● seasonal fungi ● picnic areas ● adventure play area

Sherwood Pines Forest Park

START Sherwood Pines Forest
DISTANCE 4¼ miles (6.8km)
TIME 2½ hours
PARKING Adjoining Visitor Centre (pay and display)
ROUTE FEATURES Woodland trails; gentle ascents and descents

14

This walk is at its best in the early morning or late afternoon, when the forest is quiet. Then, the chance of spotting the wildlife that abounds here is increased significantly. A gentle stroll, moving quietly through the forest glades, is the best technique and makes the experience all the more pleasurable.

A fly agaric mushroom

Leave the car park and walk towards the café and cycle hire but, before reaching it, turn right on to the start of the 'Cycle Route'.

After about 250 yds (229m), at a track junction **A**, go forward on to a footpath for walkers only, waymarked with yellow-topped poles and described as the Schools' Trail.

Soon, cross a grassy track, keeping forward, following the yellow way-marks. Continue with them as the route bends left, gently down and shortly turning left again.

Keep following the yellow trail as it passes a small pond and keep walking until the trail meets a

PUBLIC TRANSPORT Buses to Old Clipstone
REFRESHMENTS Visitor Centre café
PUBLIC TOILETS Visitor Centre
PLLAY AREA Adventure play area at rear of Visitor Centre
ORDNANCE SURVEY MAPS Explorer 28 (Sherwood Forest), Landranger 120 (Mansfield & Worksop)

wide, grassy ride. Turn right and walk out to meet a compacted forest trail at a junction.

? ***You will meet many grey squirrels on this walk, but there is one that is not real. Can you find it?***

Here B, turn right and continue to a T-junction, at which turn left. At the next junction, having just passed beneath powerlines, when the track forks, keep right (ahead).

At the next major T-junction, about 250 yds (229m) after a second

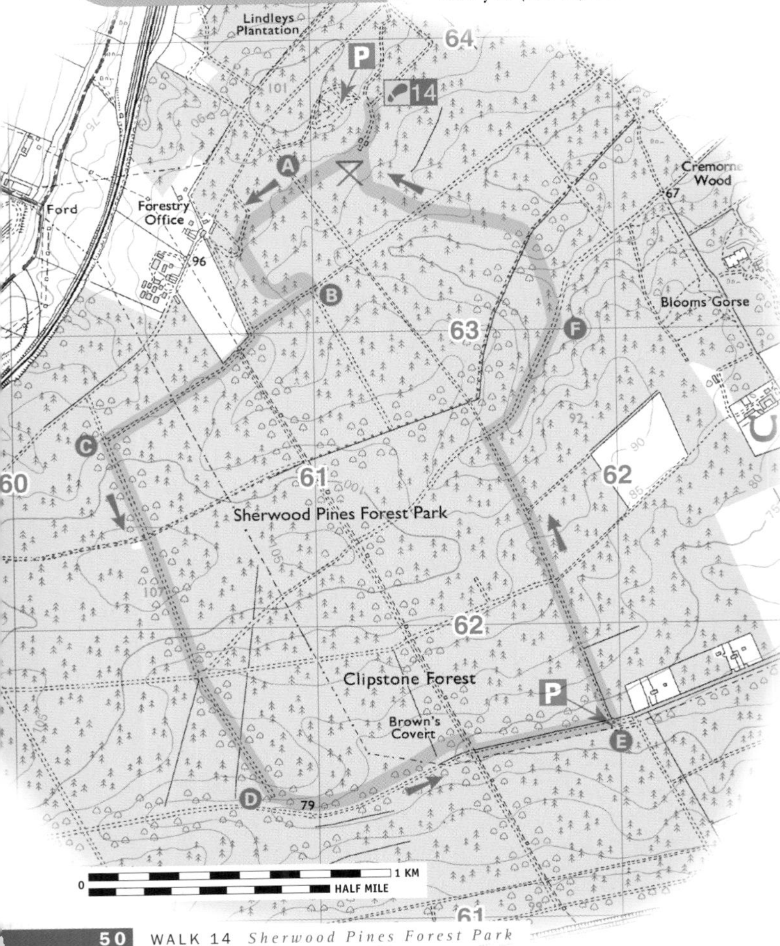

Throughout the walk, but especially as the clamour of the Visitor Centre area is left behind, keep an eye open for **woodland birds**, particularly jays, kestrels, green woodpeckers, great tits, blue tits and long-tailed tits, as well as grey squirrels. They all love this kind of habitat and live here in good numbers. They are not always easy to spot, so go quitely and keep alert.

line of overhead powerlines, turn left C. Keep forward at the next cross track, maintaining the same direction.

The next junction is a five-way. Continue ahead, keeping the same direction.

The track eventually descends to a barrier D. On reaching it, go left along a narrow footpath through bracken, roughly parallel with a slightly lower track.

Continue following the path until it emerges near a low, wooden barrier beyond which it is possible to gain the lower track. Turn left along it.

A wooden squirrel on the route

After about 400 yds (366m), at the next major turning on the left **E**, go past a barrier, rejoining the cycle trail, and now climbing gently.

At the next cross track, keep forward, following the blue cycle trail and, when this turns right, do likewise.

The track shortly reaches a wide, cleared area of forest. In the middle of this, turn left at a cross path, leaving the main forest trail.

F The path goes through a small clearing with a central pond and stands of bulrushes. A short way farther on, bear left on to a walkers' path, its course marked with blue-topped poles.

On the path through the forest park

Follow this path around a large picnic area and, when the blue trail meets the white trail, bear right around the picnic area and shortly turn left, opposite another small pond.

Continue on an obvious path (part of the white trail), walking out to intercept a wide track. Cross to the white trail diagonally opposite and follow this all the way back to the children's adventure play area, which adjoins the Visitor Centre at the starting point of the walk.

Splendid chapel • woodland wildlife • grotto

Clumber Woodlands

START Clumber
DISTANCE 4¼ miles (6.8km)
TIME 2 hours
PARKING Car park at Clumber
ROUTE FEATURES Woodland trails and paths

This tranquil walk wanders easily through the delightful woodlands of Clumber Park. The route is easy to follow, and its principal attraction is the woodland birdlife, which includes woodpeckers, owls, collared doves, jays and members of the tit family.

Walk through the car park and leave via a fence gap opposite the cycle hire building, and turn left on to a broad, estate track, soon bearing left on a track signposted to the Walled Kitchen Garden.

Continue beyond a barrier on to a surfaced estate road, passing the Clumber Conservation Centre. When this forks, branch left, following the road to a T-junction. Turn right and walk up to cross-roads at Lime Tree Avenue **A**, a beautiful avenue of double-rowed limes and a true glory in autumnal sunshine.

Keep forward into Clumber Lane (signposted to Truman's Lodge). After about 80 yds (73m), leave the road by branching right on to a path heading into woodland. When the track forks, keep on in the same direction, and, ignoring all branching paths, maintain the same direction as far as a bench about 100 yds (91m) before reaching a lane.

B Go left and walk out to rejoin Clumber Lane. Turn right as far as a pay kiosk not far from Truman's Lodge and adjacent to a sleeping policeman spanning the road.

PUBLIC TRANSPORT Buses along Lime Tree Avenue
REFRESHMENTS Restaurant at Clumber Visitor Centre
PUBLIC TOILETS At start (in shop area) and at back of conservation centre
ORDNANCE SURVEY MAPS Explorer 28 (Sherwood Forest), Landranger 120 (Mansfield & Worksop)

Immediately after this, turn acutely left on to a woodland track strewn with pine needles. Follow this, maintaining the same direction, through delightful woodland until it emerges on to a road (Lime Tree Avenue).

C Walk left for a short distance and then branch right on to a

***?** Can you discover how many people lived on the Clumber estate in Victorian times? The answer is on an information panel.*

The buildings of **Clumber Grotto** are part of the water-supply system for the park. Originally this water was pumped from an artesian well near the grotto to an underground reservoir holding 60,000 gallons (273,000 lit.) of water. This then travelled nearly ½ mile (800m) through a gravity system. The machinery is still in place, and in times of power failure can supply the park with water.

signposted footpath (a surfaced lane) for the Shop, Restaurant and Chapel.

At crossroads, turn right towards Clumber Bridge but, just before reaching the bridge, leave the road by branching left (just after a road junction) on to a woodland path that now follows the edge of Clumber Lake. The path soon reaches a fenced area at Clumber Grotto **D**.

Go past the grotto and bear right. Each time the path forks, branch right, keeping a course parallel with the lake.

The path eventually turns away from the lake and heads into the Pleasure Ground, a partially landscaped area. Go up steps and head towards a group of buildings that today house the shop and restaurant.

The area known as the **Pleasure Gardens** used to be the Italianate Gardens of Clumber House, laid out by William Sawrey Gilpin, and maintained by a team of thirty gardeners. The three rosebeds nearby stand on the site of the former fountains.

Go past the shop complex, heading out between gate pillars to reach a road. Turn right and soon reach the car park at the start. ●

St Mary's Church, Clumber

● Woodland birdlife ● attractive river ● nature reserve

16 Maun Valley and Spa Ponds

START Mansfield Woodhouse
DISTANCE 4¾ miles (7.6km)
TIME 2½–3 hours
PARKING Old Mill Lane (start of Maun Valley Trail)
ROUTE FEATURES Riverside path; wooded tracks and paths; some road walking

This walk is easy, a delightful stroll through the countryside bordering the River Maun. Hedgerowed ancient highways, once used by merchants travelling to and from markets, lead through riparian scenes that are captivating at any time of year. In autumn, keep an eye out for the winter thrushes – brambling, fieldfare and visiting mistle thrush.

The **River Maun** can provide glimpses of kingfishers or a patrolling heron. It flows through the centre of the market town of **Mansfield**, at the heart of the ancient Sherwood Forest. Later, the town became important for spinning cotton, with the river supporting at least ten mills. When cotton production declined, Mansfield developed into one of Britain's most important coal-mining centres.

Leave the car park through a stile giving into an elongated field, and follow a path through this to a stone arched bridge. Cross the bridge and bear right, following a clear path across a wide, grassy corridor, and eventually reaching a road (New Mill Lane).

Go into the right-hand of two tracks opposite, a signposted

Whinney Hill Woodland is a narrow and elongated stretch of ash, hazel, sycamore, birch, hawthorn, oak and holly, bordered by well-established hedgerows. In spring, visiting warblers join the resident finches and various members of the tit family, while later in the year large flocks of yellowhammer, linnets and goldfinches may be seen both here and across the adjacent farmland.

PUBLIC TRANSPORT Buses along Old Mill Lane
REFRESHMENTS Pub at Newlands
PUBLIC TOILETS None on route
ORDNANCE SURVEY MAPS Explorer 28 (Sherwood Forest), Landranger 120 (Mansfield & Worksop)

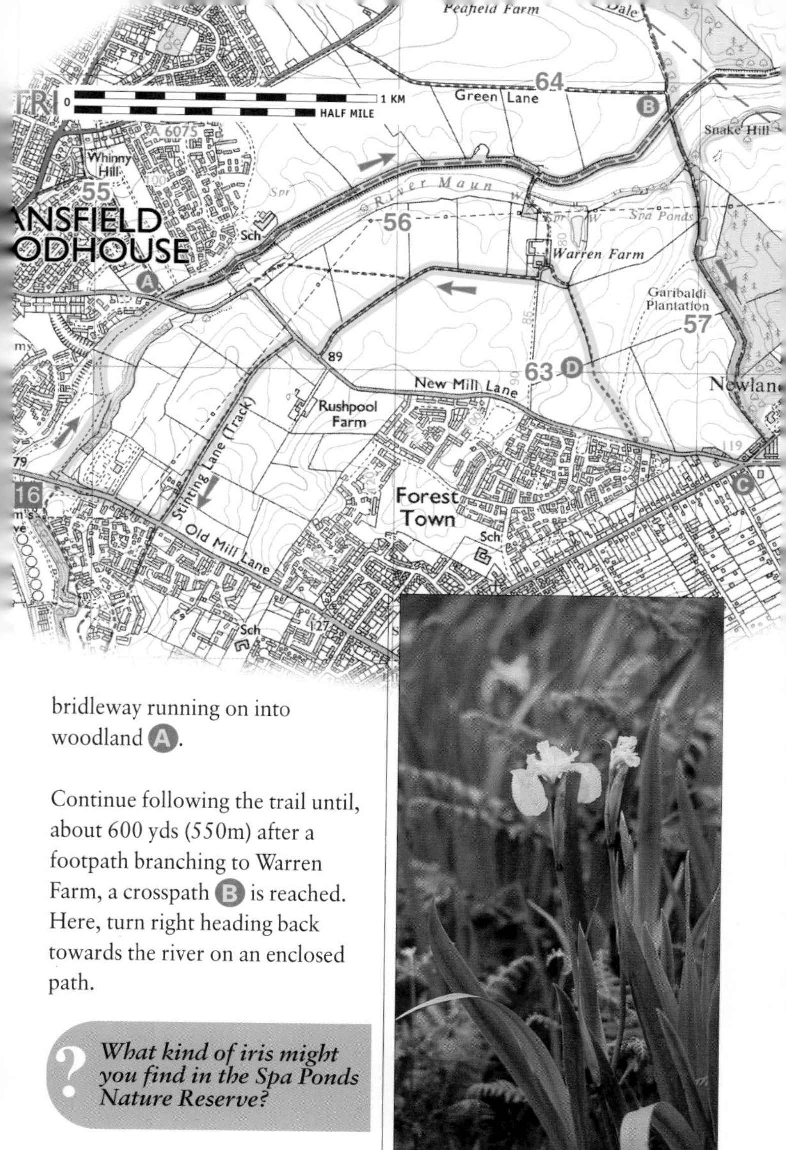

bridleway running on into woodland A.

Continue following the trail until, about 600 yds (550m) after a footpath branching to Warren Farm, a crosspath B is reached. Here, turn right heading back towards the river on an enclosed path.

> ? *What kind of iris might you find in the Spa Ponds Nature Reserve?*

Cross the river and beyond climb gently to reach the first of a series

Yellow flag irises in Spa Ponds

of small ponds at the entrance to the Spa Ponds Nature Reserve.

Keep following the path beyond the Spa Ponds until it emerges at a road. Turn right to a major junction at Newlands, and there turn immediately right into New Mill Lane (signposted to Mansfield and Woodhouse) C.

Cross New Mill Lane to the footpath on the left-hand side and continue down the road for about 350 yds (320m) to a signposted foot-path on the right.

The trail runs along the edge of **woodland** containing some different species from the earlier track. Here Scots pine puts in an appearance, along with elder, birch, the locally common Spanish chestnut and the invasive Himalayan balsam, the pink-to-white flowers of which give it the nickname Policeman's Helmet. The balsam is also known as Jumping Jack after the way its seed pods explode when gently squeezed.

The path gives into a large open field and follows a well-trodden course. The much-used appearance of the path can cause confusion, however, because it heads in the wrong direction. So, a few strides after it is joined from the left by another path, leave the clear path for a much less distinct one on the left, ascending a gentle

Snowdrops in the woodland

On the Maun Valley Trail

field slope and climbing to a hedge corner at the top.

D From the hedge corner, go forward through the remains of an old hedgerow to continue ahead, with a hedgerow on the left. This is a useful guide to Warren Farm.

The path descends towards the farm and, as it does so, bear left and then right towards a red-brick farm building.

Keep to the left of the farm buildings to walk past them to the farm access, a surfaced track. Follow this until it reaches New Mill Lane again. Turn right.

Take care against approaching traffic and, after about 100 yds (91m), turn left into a hedgerowed track (Stinting Lane) and follow this until it meets Old Mill Lane.

Turn right again and walk down the lane to return to the start of the Maun Valley Trail, where this walk began.

Spa Ponds Nature Reserve was established in 1984 and comprises three spring-fed medieval ponds and a modern pond, all surrounded by woodland. Springs and ponds are rare in this area because of the porous nature of the bedrock, Sherwood sandstone.

The ponds support a variety of aquatic plants and animals and are noted for dragonfly, iris and water-lilies. Bird species here include coot, little grebe and the occasional kingfisher. In the surrounding woodland, which is oak-dominated, hedgehogs, voles, foxes and weasels can also be found.

• Woodland wildlife • ancient tree • attractive river • 12th-century church

17 Birklands and Edwinstowe

The main feature of this delightful circuit is the amazing range of wildlife that makes the woodland its home. A quiet approach and a pair of binoculars make the walk much more pleasurable but has the effect of extending the time taken.

START Sherwood Forest Visitor Centre
DISTANCE 5½ miles (8.9km)
TIME 2½–3 hours
PARKING Adjoining Visitor Centre
ROUTE FEATURES Woodland trails; roads; riverside path

Sherwood Forest was made a Site of Special Scientific Interest (SSSI) in 1954. It is the last remaining part of the old Sherwood Forest of medieval times and has one of the best examples of oak and birch woodland in the country. The old oaks and birch provide homes and food for a host of creatures, especially insects.

Leave the car park and walk towards the Visitor Centre, going past it on a broad pathway sign-posted to the Major Oak.

Continue to follow the path for Major Oak but, before reaching the oak tree, leave the path at a bridle-way **A** crossing left and right and accessed by gates. Turn right and shortly cross another track, but continue to follow the bridleway (waymarked green, red and yellow).

When the path next forks, continue with the red and yellow trail, keeping forward through beautiful stands of birch and oak.

At the next junction go ahead, still on the bridleway, and now accessing the Dukeries Training

PUBLIC TRANSPORT Buses to Visitor Centre
REFRESHMENTS Café in Visitor Centre; pubs and cafés in Edwinstowe
PUBLIC TOILETS Adjoining Visitor Centre
PLAY AREA Near car park
ORDNANCE SURVEY MAPS Explorer 28 (Sherwood Forest), Landranger 120 (Mansfield & Worksop)

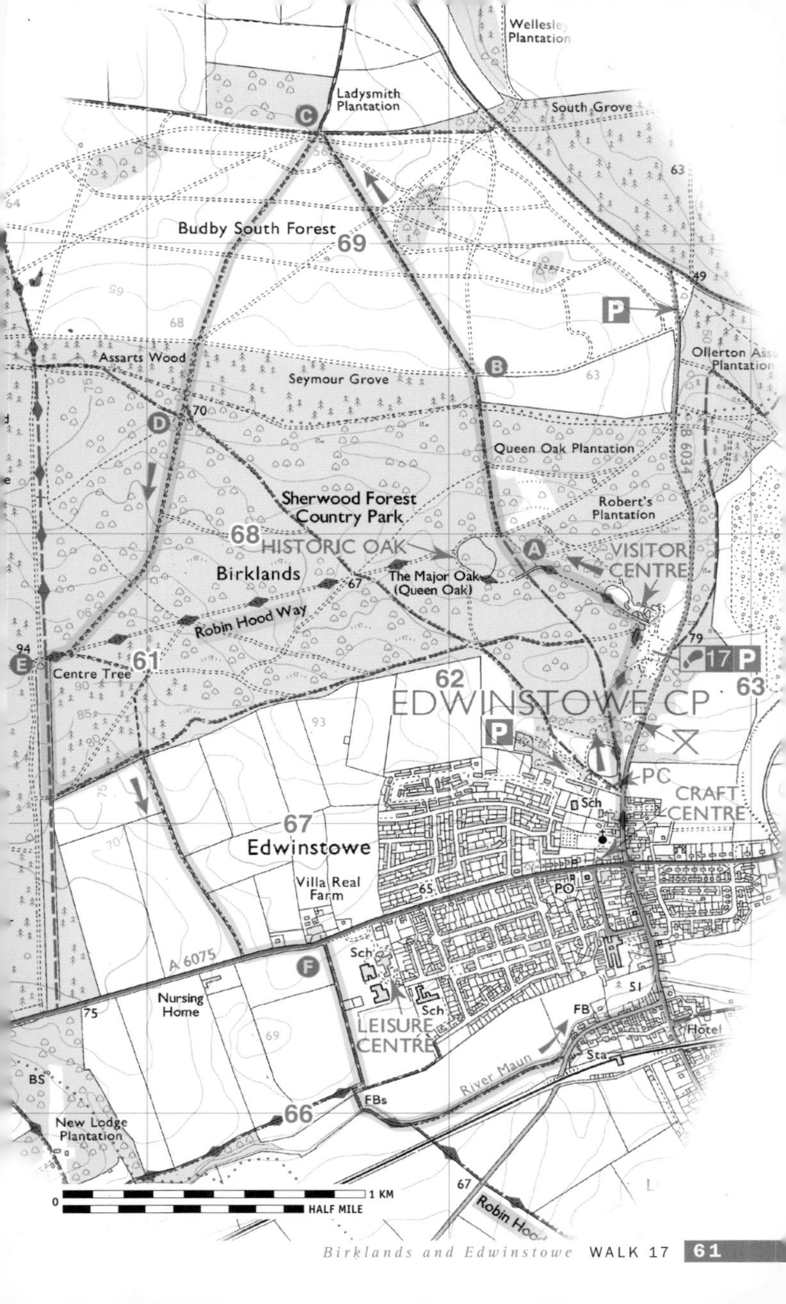
Ladysmith Plantation
South Grove
Budby South Forest
Assarts Wood
Seymour Grove
Ollerton Assarts Plantation
Queen Oak Plantation
Sherwood Forest Country Park
Robert's Plantation
HISTORIC OAK
VISITOR CENTRE
Birklands
The Major Oak (Queen Oak)
Robin Hood Way
Centre Tree
EDWINSTOWE CP
PC
CRAFT CENTRE
Sch
Edwinstowe
Villa Real Farm
PO
A 6075
Nursing Home
LEISURE CENTRE
FB
Hotel
Sta
River Maun
FBs
BS
New Lodge Plantation
B 6034
1 KM
HALF MILE

> ? *Can you discover who was a 'True Free Spirit'?*

Area **B**. Go past a metal barrier and continue on a narrow footpath (no longer waymarked). It is important to keep to the right-of-way here as the adjacent land forms part of a military training area.

The bridleway soon crosses a broad forest trail and immediately forks. Here branch left and follow a sandy path for over ½ mile (800m) to intercept another broad track near Ladysmith Plantation and at a track junction.

Ignore all the prominent tracks and instead bear sharply left into an enclosed track **C** heading back for the distant confines of the forest.

Back within the boundary of Sherwood Forest, cross a broad track and keep forward. After about 200 yds (183m) cross another track and keep forward, soon branching right when the path forks. This shortly intercepts a bridleway **D**.

Continue ahead, maintaining the same direction on a waymarked public footpath (yellow waymark). The path eventually joins another. Keep right and walk out to a metal barrier, beyond which turn immediately left on to a broad forest ride. At the head of the ride stands the Centre Tree **E**, a massive oak that marked the boundaries between the dukedoms of Welbeck and Newcastle, and is said to mark the centre of the ancient Sherwood Forest.

Mixed woodland of Birklands, the heart of Sherwood

Head down the ride, flanked on one side by broadleaved woodland and holly and on the other by conifers. Continue for 500 yds (457m) to a bench and signposted bridleway.

Turn left on to a pathway that runs along the forest edge, with arable land on the right. When the path forks, keep right.

After about 300 yds (274m), leave the forest trail by turning right on to a sign-posted footpath enclosed between a hedgerow and a fence. Follow the path, later unenclosed and running along field edges to meet the A6075.

Sherwood is renowned for its fungi

Turn left along the roadside footpath, but after 300 yds (274m) cross the road with care and turn into a wide vehicle track (just after reaching Mansfield Road) F. When the track bends right, turn with it for about 20 yds (18m) and then go left through a hedge gap and forward to a footbridge spanning the River Maun.

After the footbridge a narrow path pleasantly parallels the course of the river and leads out to meet a road (Mill Lane). Turn left and follow the road to a T-junction.

Turn left and then walk up towards Edwinstowe. On entering the village, as the main road bends left, go forward against a one-way system and walk up High Street to traffic lights at the junction with the A6075.

Keep forward into Church Street, passing on the way the Church of St Mary.

Continue to Forest Corner, and there go forward on to a signposted path at the edge of Sherwood Forest Country Park, following the route for the Visitor Centre.

Beyond a cricket field, as the path forks, keep right. At the next path junction turn right and go past a children's play area to reach the centre car park at the start of the walk.

St Mary's Church dates from the 12th and 14th centuries, and stands on the site of an earlier church dating from the 7th century, believed to have been built on the site where King Edwin of Northumbria was buried in 633 AD. Legend has it that it was in this church that Robin Hood married Maid Marian.

18 Greasley and Beauvale

A delightful wander through the beautiful woodlands and stunning landscapes of D.H. Lawrence country. This is a walk that rewards a steady and patient approach, ambling pleasurably along, taking in the rolling farmland scenery and the fine, distant views of hilltop churches.

START Moorgreen
DISTANCE 6 miles (9.7km)
TIME 2½–3 hours
PARKING Colliers Wood
ROUTE FEATURES Woodland trails; muddy farm fields; a few awkward stiles

Begin from the car park at Colliers Wood, the site – unbelievably to look at the place today – of Moorgreen Colliery, which for more than ten years mined over a million tons of coal.

Walk across the car park and through a kissing-gate, soon bearing left when the path forks.

Continue following the path to a T-junction, and there turn right, following the Blackshale Trail. This leads to a wooden barrier, immediately after which you should turn left through a kissing-gate and walk up the left-hand edge of an arable field.

Today **Colliers Wood** is a community woodland, forming part of the Greenwood Community Forest in Nottinghamshire. The name was chosen through a local competition, and the site was designed to restore the woodlands and fields that existed before Moorgreen Colliery was opened.

At the top of a field go left over a stile into a narrow field, and then bear right through a gap on to a grassy pathway intermittently flanked by hawthorn.

PUBLIC TRANSPORT Buses to Moorgreen and Greasley
REFRESHMENTS Tearoom at Greasley
PUBLIC TOILETS None on route
ORDNANCE SURVEY MAPS Explorer 260 (Nottingham, Vale of Belvoir), Landranger 129 (Nottingham & Loughborough)

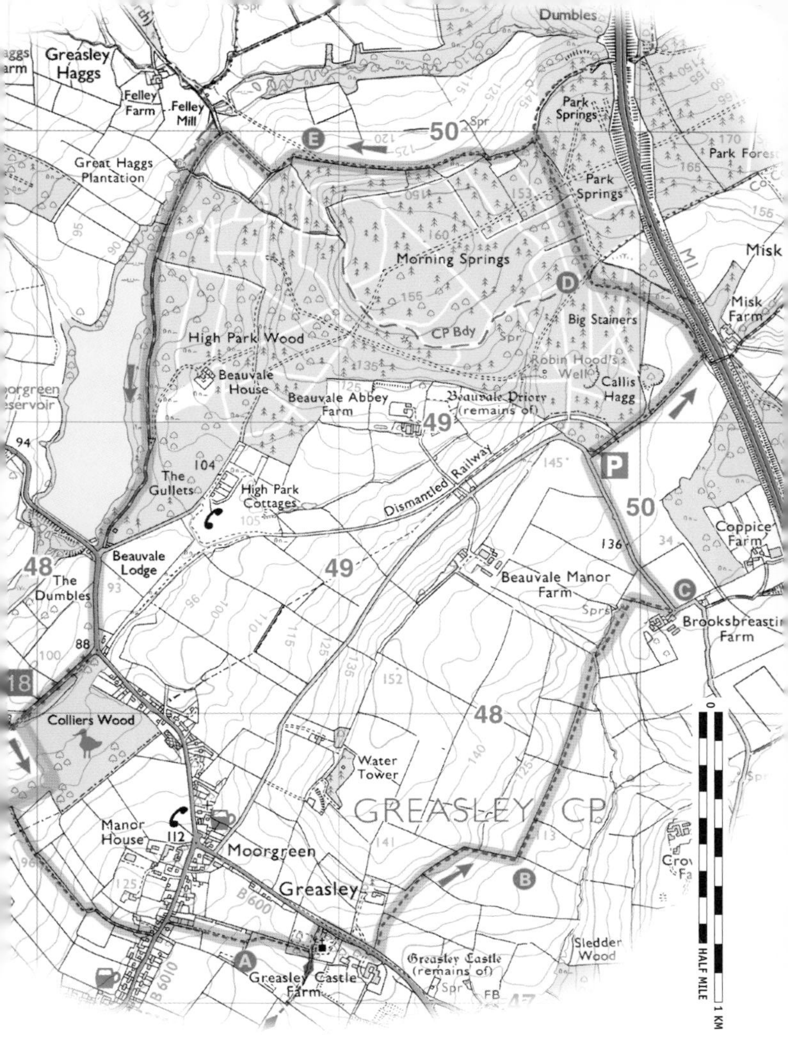

Follow the path out to meet a road and turn left for a short distance to a signposted turning on the right, which is a vehicle track for Greasley Church.

Keep heading for the church, leaving the stony track eventually by turning left to a kissing-gate **A** and going up the ensuing field towards the church.

The site of Moorgreen Colliery, Colliers Wood

Another kissing-gate gives into the churchyard. Go forward towards the church and, just before reaching it, turn left on a path that leads out to meet the B600.

Turn right along the B600 for about 200 yds (183m), then leave the road by turning over a stile on the left (near an information panel). Walk up the left-hand edge of two fields. At the top of the second field, continue to follow the field boundary, round a corner and into another field.

A field boundary path leads down to a sign-post **B**. Here turn left, continuing to follow a field edge. In the corner of the field, cross a narrow footbridge and go forward across the next field to locate another footbridge spanning Gilt Brook.

In the ensuing field, turn left along a field boundary on a path that leads into and across a small pasture. In the next field, turn immediately right and walk out to meet a lane at a bend. Turn left **C**.

Walk up the road as far as a parking area on the right and here turn right on to a signposted path for Hucknall.

The path eventually breaks out into

The church is dedicated to **St Mary** and stands on the site of a church mentioned in the 'Domesday Book'. It was a favourite haunt of D.H. Lawrence, who portrayed it as Willey Green Church in *Women in Love.*

In the 14th century, Greasley was a parish of considerable importance as Nicholas de Cantelupe, lord of Greasley and a distinguished soldier, settled here in his manor-house. The house adjoined the church and was fortified to become Greasley Castle.

? *Which childhood friend of D.H. Lawrence encouraged him to write and was immortalised as Miriam in* Sons and Lovers?

a large arable field. Follow the field edge, passing for a short while close by the M1 motorway, but eventually finding a way into the relative peace of woodland.

This is the landscape that **D.H. Lawrence** loved so much. He was born in 1885 in the nearby town of Eastwood. Lawrence used the characters and events of the area as inspiration for his works. His father was a miner who worked at Brinsley, the sister pit of Moorgreen. Many of Lawrence's novels are set around Eastwood, and mining features prominently in his work.

Turn left, following a lovely path that finally emerges at a forest track. Turn right and walk along the forest trail until it forks **D**. Here, ignore both forest trails, and instead go ahead on to a narrow path back into mixed woodland, in due course emerging at the top of a large sloping pasture.

Turn left along a path at the top of the pasture, with the woodland boundary on the left, and stunning views ahead.

Keep following the boundary path until, as it swerves away to the right **E**, a narrow (signposted) path maintains faith with the woodland for a while longer. Follow this, as it bends left and goes down to another signpost. Here turn right along the line of an old hedgerow, now comprising oak, hawthorn and holly.

At the bottom of the field, bear left to a stile giving on to a woodland bridleway (signed for Moorgreen). Turn left along the bridleway and follow its delightful course through woodland flanking Moorgreen Reservoir, finally reaching a surfaced lane and walking out to Beauvale Lodge near the B600.

Turn left and walk along a roadside footpath, shortly turning right into Engine Lane (signposted for Colliers Wood), only a short distance for the start of the walk. ●

Farming landscape at Greasley

● Attractive village ● farmland landscape ● woodlands ● viewpoint

19 *Farnsfield and Robin Hood Hill*

START Farnsfield
DISTANCE 6¼ miles (10.1km)
TIME 3 hours
PARKING Roadside, next to church
ROUTE FEATURES Farmland; woodland; hills; stiles

Taking an idyllic course across sweeping landscapes of farmland, this walk teases a way through to Robin Hood Hill, a fine viewpoint, before returning to the village of Farnsfield. Wildlife is at a premium, but it is for the views that this walk is undertaken, and they are outstanding. The walk may be shortened by 2 miles (3.2km).

From the church walk left into Blidworth Road and left again into Church Side, going forward alongside a wall, on part of Robin Hood Way. The path emerges at a lane.

Cross, and go through two kissing-gates opposite and across two fields on a grassy path. At the top of the second field, pass through two more kissing-gates and half-left to enter an enclosed path a short distance away. This leads out to a lane (Combs Lane). Turn right A.

A short distance along Combs Lane, a branching lane is signed to the Halifax Bomber Memorial. This is an optional addition to the walk of about 600 yds (549m). Simply turn down the lane to reach the memorial, set in a gated area. The memorial commemorates the crew of Halifax Bomber MZ519 LK-U of 578 Squadron who died here at Farnsfield on 6 July 1944 returning from operations.

Continue along Combs Lane until about 100 yds (91m) before a turning to Combs Farm, at a gap on the left B. The Robin Hood Way leaves the track and then heads diagonally across the

PUBLIC TRANSPORT Buses to Farnsfield
REFRESHMENTS Pubs in Farnsfield
PUBLIC TOILETS None on route
ORDNANCE SURVEY MAPS Explorer 28 (Sherwood Forest), Landranger 120 (Mansfield & Worksop)

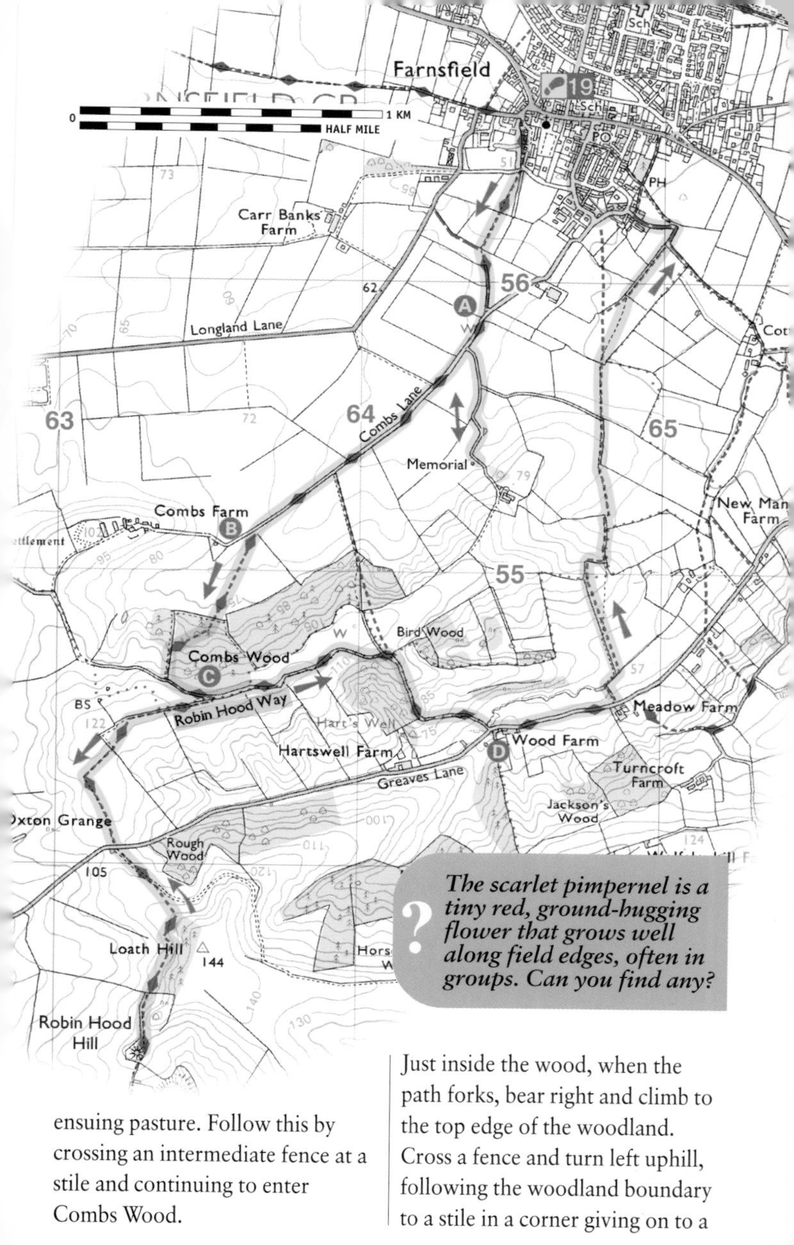

The scarlet pimpernel is a tiny red, ground-hugging flower that grows well along field edges, often in groups. Can you find any?

ensuing pasture. Follow this by crossing an intermediate fence at a stile and continuing to enter Combs Wood.

Just inside the wood, when the path forks, bear right and climb to the top edge of the woodland. Cross a fence and turn left uphill, following the woodland boundary to a stile in a corner giving on to a broad track. Over the stile, turn left again.

The Halifax bomber memorial

Follow the track as far as a footpath turning on the right, which is signposted to Oxton **C**. Here begins the section of the walk to Robin Hood Hill. (If you wish, this out-and-back section can be omitted. Doing this will save 2 miles/3.4km.)

Turn right through a hedge gap and walk around the boundary of two fields as far as another hedge gap (waymark). Turn through the gap and along a grassy path as far as an isolated oak tree in mid-field, besides which stands a waymark pole. Turn left here.

Cross an arable field to a stile giving on to a lane. Cross the lane and the stile opposite to walk up a broad field track as far as a way-mark pole and here bear right, climbing to the corner of a small copse cloaking Loath Hill.

Bear right along the copse edge, continuing as far as a stile giving into a sloping field. Go forward alongside a fence, passing the first hill, adorned by a few oak trees, to reach a second, bare of any adornment. This is Robin Hood Hill, and the view from it is excellent.

Here you have a choice of routes. Either retrace the outward route back to the edge of Combs Wood, re-entering the wood and turning right along a broad track, or, from the top of Robin Hood Hill, go back to the stile and along the woodland boundary, later turning left to rejoin the field track out to the lane.

Cross the lane and the ensuing field to a mid-field oak, and there turn right to a hedge gap. Go through the gap and turn left to walk around the field boundary as far as the Oxton signpost. Here turn right on to a woodland track.

Continue along the track, which wanders pleasantly through a narrow corridor of woodland to meet a footpath sign. Ignore this and turn right down a sunken track, slippery and awkward in places, until it finally emerges at a road (Greaves Lane) **D**.

Turn left for nearly ¼ mile (400m) and then leave Greaves Lane by turning left on to a descending vehicle track that leads into a rising pasture. Turn right to a field corner and left up the field edge (ignoring a hedge gap) for about 100 yds (91m). At a powerline pole, switch sides of the hedge and continue climbing, now with a hedge on the left.

Cross the top of the ascent and follow the field boundary round to a waymarked stile in a field corner.

Continue down the ensuing field, targeting the steeple of Farnsfield Church and maintaining an obvious route across a succession of fields, always following the same direction.

Go across the edge of a sports field giving on to a broad track. Keep ahead and follow this around a bend to enter a housing estate (Cotton Mill Lane). At the end of the lane, turn left (Quaker Lane) and, at Tippings Lane, turn right.

Walk up to the main street in Farnsfield and turn left to return to the church at the start.

An oak on the way to the village of Farnsfield

20 Eakring and Robin Hood Way

START Eakring
DISTANCE 6½ miles (10.5km)
TIME 3 hours
PARKING Savile Arms car park (please park at top end of car park and do not obstruct barn doors)
ROUTE FEATURES Woodland trails; farm paths; a few stiles; some mud

The attractive village of Eakring sits at the centre of its parish, seemingly untroubled by the affairs of the world. All around, farming landscapes extend as far as the eye can see, to Lincoln Cathedral on a good day, and it is these easy-on-the-eye vistas, the acres of sky and the birdlife that make this walk so agreeable. Allow more time if you wish to visit the nature reserve.

Leave the pub car park and walk out to the main road, crossing to enter Church Lane. When the lane bends left, leave it and go forward alongside cottages to a signpost at the edge of a farm field.

Strike out across the field and, on the other side, ignore a stile and bear right on a field-edge path to another stile further on.

Over the stile, walk along a narrow path through undergrowth and, at its end, go forward into Side Lane and out to the main road. Turn right.

? *Some of the old oil pumps used in Duke's Wood have been restored. Can you find out what their nickname was?*

Follow the road until it bends left and there leave it by going forward in Brail Lane. After the last of a row of houses the lane becomes a broad, grassy track along a field edge.

On reaching a field track, turn left along it until, about 150 yds (137m) from a woodland edge, it forks. Here turn left and walk out to meet the road again.

PUBLIC TRANSPORT Buses to Eakring
REFRESHMENTS Savile Arms
PUBLIC TOILETS None on route (Savile Arms, patrons only)
ORDNANCE SURVEY MAPS Explorer 28 (Sherwood Forest), Landranger 120 (Mansfield & Worksop)

Turn right and follow the road, taking care against approaching traffic, until about 200 yds (183m) after the entrance to Coultas Farm, where the road can be left in favour of a broad track on the left **A**.

The parish church at Eakring

When the track makes a pronounced bend to the left, leave it by going forward at a waymark (yellow and the symbol for the Robin Hood Way, which is now followed all the way back to Eakring). Continue forward on a leafy path flanked by field maple, oak, ash and blackthorn (which in autumn are still heavy with sloes).

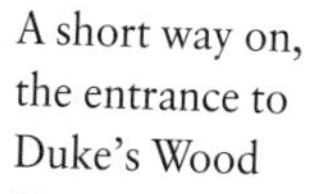

A short way on, the entrance to Duke's Wood Nature Reserve is reached. The walk does not go through the reserve, but with time in hand a diversion into the reserve is well worthwhile.

Duke's Wood and the area around it was the location of Britain's first onshore oilfield, which produced 280,000 tons of oil between 1939 and 1966. The wood is dominated by oak, ash, hazel and birch, and a few remaining elm. It provides a habitat for a wide range of birds that in summer include blackcap, garden warbler and spotted flycatcher, and great spotted woodpecker and jay throughout the year as well as the occasional hawfinch. In winter, small flocks of long-tailed tits and willow tits frequent the trees. Nightingales breed here, and can be heard singing their evocative song during April and May.

The path maintains a delightful course through a narrow strip of woodland and eventually emerges in the corner of a large field **B**. Here turn left over a narrow footbridge and go ahead along the right-hand edge of the ensuing field.

The path parallels a woodland boundary and 'dips' into the next field to continue along a field edge.

Eventually, the boundary path meets another, where you turn left towards a hedge gap. Through this, turn left following a field edge to Holywell Farm.

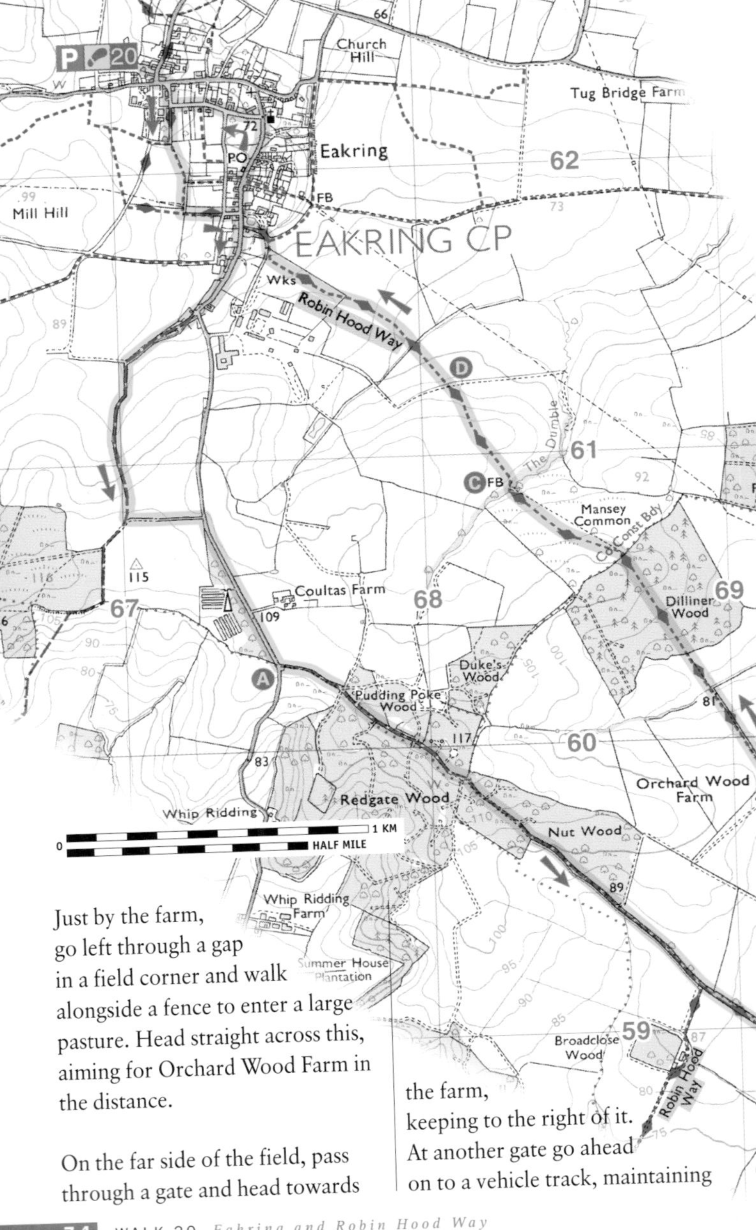

Just by the farm, go left through a gap in a field corner and walk alongside a fence to enter a large pasture. Head straight across this, aiming for Orchard Wood Farm in the distance.

On the far side of the field, pass through a gate and head towards the farm, keeping to the right of it. At another gate go ahead on to a vehicle track, maintaining the same direction, and descending gently to a field gate before crossing a pasture to the confines of Dilliner Wood.

The way through the woodland, which is often muddy but quite delightful, is clear and waymarked throughout. It leads, with imperceptible change, into the less woody, more scrubby confines of Mansey Common, where the path is less distinct but never in doubt. Finally, it drops to an open-sided footbridge **C** spanning the Dumble, climbs steps on the other side and emerges into the edge of a huge field.

Head out into the field, where the direction is usually clear enough (except when the field has just been ploughed). The path climbs steadily and at its high point brings St Andrew's Church in Eakring into view, which proves a useful target. Head now downfield to a waymark in a hedgerow **D**.

Cross a field track and go through a hedge gap, continuing to follow a path across two more fields.

On the far side of the second field, walk through a gap in a hedge and forward along a field edge. In the field corner, turn right into another field but then turn immediately left on to a grassy path that leads out to a road.

Turn right and walk as far as the parish church. Opposite the church, turn into Church Lane. Follow this until it meets the outward route. From there retrace the route to the start.

Hedged woodland path

Further Information

Walking Safety

Although the reasonably gentle countryside that is the subject of this book offers no real dangers to walkers at any time of the year, it is still advisable to take sensible precautions and follow certain well-tried guidelines.

Always take with you both warm and waterproof clothing and sufficient food and drink. Wear suitable footwear, i.e. strong walking boots or shoes that give a good grip over stony ground, on slippery slopes and in muddy conditions. Try to obtain a local weather forecast and bear it in mind before you start. Do not be afraid to abandon your proposed route and return to your starting point in the event of a sudden and unexpected deterioration in the weather.

All the walks described in this book will be safe to do, given due care and respect, even during the winter. Indeed, a crisp, fine winter day often provides perfect walking conditions, with firm ground underfoot and a clarity unique to this time of the year.

The most difficult hazard likely to be encountered is mud, especially

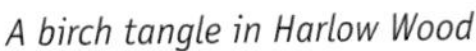

A birch tangle in Harlow Wood

when walking along woodland and field paths, farm tracks and bridleways – the latter in particular can often get churned up by cyclists and horses. In summer, an additional difficulty may be narrow and overgrown paths, particularly along the edges of cultivated fields. Neither should constitute a major problem, provided that the appropriate footwear is worn.

The River Meden at Church Warsop

Follow the Country Code

- Enjoy the countryside and respect its life and work
- Guard against all risk of fire
- Take your litter home
- Fasten all gates
- Help to keep all water clean
- Keep your dogs under control
- Protect wildlife, plants and trees
- Keep to public paths across farmland
- Take special care on country roads
- Leave livestock, crops and machinery alone
- Make no unnecessary noise
- Use gates and stiles to cross fences, hedges and walls

(The Countryside Agency)

Useful organisations

Council for the Protection of Rural England
Warwick House, 25 Buckingham Palace Road, London SW1W 0PP.
Tel. 020 7976 6433
E-mail: cpre@gn.apc.org

Countryside Agency
John Dower House, Crescent Place, Cheltenham GL50 3RA.
Tel. 01242 521381;
Fax 01242 584270;
www.countryside.gov.uk

East Midlands Tourist Board
Exchequergate, Lincoln LN2 1PZ.
Tel. 01522 531521;
Fax 01522 532501

English Heritage
23 Savile Row,
London W1X 1AB.
Tel. 020 7973 3434;
Fax 020 7973 3001;
www.english-heritage.org.uk

English Nature
Northminster House,
Peterborough,
Cambridgeshire
PE1 1UA.
Tel. 01733 455100;
Fax 01733 455103; E-mail:
enquiries@english-nature.org.uk;
www.english-nature.org.uk

Forestry Commission
Information Branch,
231 Corstorphine Road,
Edinburgh
EH12 7AT.
Tel. 0131 334 0303

National Trust
Membership and general enquiries:
PO Box 39, Bromley,
Kent BR1 3XL.
Tel. 020 8315 1111
E-mail:enquiries@ntrust.org.uk
East Midlands Regional Office:
Clumber Park Stableyard,
Worksop,
Nottinghamshire
S80 3BE.
Tel. 01909 486411
Fax 01909 486377

Nottinghamshire County Council
Tourism and County Parks Service
Rufford Abbey, Ollerton,
Nottinghamshire NG22 9DF.
Tel. 01623 822944, ext. 220/221/
237; www.nottinghamshiretourism.
co.uk

Ordnance Survey
Romsey Road, Maybush,
Southampton SO16 4GU.
Tel. 08456 05 05 05 (Lo-call)
E-mail: custinfo@ordsvy.gov.uk;
www.ordsvy.gov.uk

Public transport
Bus Traveline: 0870 608 2608

Ramblers' Association
2nd Floor, Camelford House,
87–90 Albert Embankment,
London SE1 7TW.
Tel. 020 7339 8500;
Fax 020 7339 8501;
www.ramblers.org.uk

Royal Society for the Protection of Birds (RSPB)
The Lodge, Sandy,
Bedfordshire SG19 2DL.
Tel. 01767 680551;
Fax 01767 692365;
www.rspb.org.uk

Tourist information centres:
Mansfield: 01623 824545
Newark-on-Trent: 01636 655765

Nottingham: 0115 915 5330;
E-mail: tourist.information
@nottinghamcity.gov.uk
Ollerton: 01623 824545
Retford: 01777 860780
Sherwood Forest Visitor Centre, Edwinstowe: 01623 824490
West Bridford: 0115 977 3558
Workshop: 01909 501148

Youth Hostels Association
Trevelyan House, Dimple Road
Matlock, Derbyshire DE4 3YH
Tel. 01629 592600
Website: www.yha.org.uk

Ordnance Survey Maps of Nottingham and Sherwood Forest

Explorer maps 28 (Sherwood Forest), 260 (Nottingham, Vale of Belvoir) and Landranger maps 120 (Mansfield & Worksop), 129 (Nottingham & Loughborough).

Answers to Questions

Walk 1: Bluebells. On the walk towards the abbey ruins there is a bench 'In Loving Memory of Norma Mary Roddis 1935–1996 who loved the bluebells'.
Walk 2: Great, blue, coal, willow and long-tailed tits can all be encountered. A basic birdwatching manual is always a useful item to carry on woodland walks.
Walk 3: She was also a city councillor. The bench is at the head of the avenue of lime trees.
Walk 4: It lies along the final section of the Robin Hood Way, met with on the walk, and marks the spot where the first British specimen of an Egyptian nightjar was spotted in 1883.
Walk 5: Bison and reindeer.
Walk 6: A man and a towing horse. At the start of the walk there is a quotation from *The Rainbow*, in which Lawrence writes, '... the canal embankment, which rose like a high rampart near at hand, so that occasionally, a man's figure

Along the Maun Valley Trail

passed in silhouette, or a man and a towing horse traversed the sky.'

Walk 7: Long-tailed tit. These lovely birds are present all year, but tend to flock together into small groups in winter. A basic field guide to birds and a pair of binoculars are always useful items to take on a walk.

Walk 8: The tree is the yew, a long-lived evergreen. The churchyard yew probably stems from a pre-Christian belief that they sheltered a protective deity or spirit, and so were planted to ward off evil spirits.

Walk 9: 20.

Walk 10: The symbol of both birds is imprinted into the top of the waymark poles along the bank of the River Trent.

Walk 11: Cockpen Tree, a reference to its use as a cockerel pen during the mid-18th century. Game-birds were stacked inside the tree in wicker baskets or tied in hessian sacks before they were released and used for the now illegal sport of cockfighting.

Walk 12: She was the Duchess of Newcastle, and her ashes were scattered from Clumber Bridge on 1 October 1997.

Walk 13: It is a moorhen. A simple birdwatcher's guide will help to identify many of the birds found on this and other walks.

Walk 14: A small wooden squirrel stands just to one side of the Schools' Trail in the first part of the walk.

Walk 15: 500; in Hardwick village, on the farm, in the gate lodges, the house and its surrounding buildings. The information is on a panel near the grotto.

Walk 16: Yellow flag iris, which are especially suited to this kind of habitat. Have a look at the information panel where the Spa Ponds track finally emerges on a road at Newlands.

Walk 17: Janet Clarkson – the bench along the forest ride south of the Centre Tree is to her memory.

Walk 18: Jessie Chambers. Information is given on the panel near Greasley Church.

Walk 19: Scarlet pimpernel can be found in many places, but they favour ploughed fields, and can be found along the section of the walk out to Robin Hood Hill.

Walk 20: Nodding donkeys. You can glimpse some from the main route, and information is given about them on the information panel at the entrance to the reserve.